Creative Intelligence

and Self-Liberation

*Korzybski, Non-Aristotelian Thinking
and Eastern Realization*

Ted Falconar

Crown House Publishing

www.crownhouse.co.uk

First published by

Crown House Publishing Ltd
Crown Buildings, Bancyfelin, Carmarthen, Wales, SA33 5ND, UK
www.crownhouse.co.uk

and

Crown House Publishing Ltd
P.O. Box 2223, Williston, VT 05495-2223, USA
www.CHPUS.com

British Library of Cataloguing-in-Publication Data
A catalogue entry for this book is available
from the British Library.

ISBN 1899836497

LCCN 2003114977

Illustrated by Charlotte Henry

Printed on-demand and bound by
Antony Rowe Ltd
Eastbourne

A tribute by the author:

Count Alfred Korzybski

Born Warsaw, Poland, 1879

Died U.S.A., 1950

The greatest philosophical idea that ever came out of India
2500–3000 years ago is Realization (how to see reality).

Despite knowing nothing about Eastern thought, Korzybski
produced in ten years a far more comprehensive and logical
exposition of Realization, calling it Non-Aristotelian Thinking.

This was the work of a supreme genius, yet he remains largely
unknown and neglected.

My book is to encourage some posthumous recognition of this
great mind, whose work transformed my life; and to clarify and
explain what is a difficult subject for many people.

Ted Falconar

Being myself a remarkably stupid fellow, I have had to unteach myself the difficulties, and now beg to present to my fellow fools the parts that are not hard. Master these thoroughly, and the rest will follow. What one fool can do, another can!

– Sylvanus P. Thompson
Calculus Made Easy

Little children live in a technicolour and sense world until words replace their senses. Then joy ends and the colours fade into a black and white world of words.

This book teaches how to regain our senses and return to that original world, which is also the way Albert Einstein and geniuses think.

Contents

Ted Falconar

Ted Falconar was born in Darjeeling, India, where his father had a tea estate. In accordance with his Scots-English ancestry, he was schooled in Scotland and England. He went to the Indian Military Academy at Dehra Dun following in the steps of his brother who was killed with the 10th Gurkhas in Burma. He, however, served not with the 10th Gurkhas but with the Burma Rifles. After the Second World War he was a tea planter in Darjeeling until Indian Independence when he went to London to learn tea tasting. Next he went to America where he managed tea packing factories and tasted tea. Back in England he applied his lifelong interest in philosophy and human relations to managing companies. Ideas enabling workers to fulfil their potential and to harness their creativity were so successful that Tetley Tea Company, of which he was Managing Director, was turned round so that its productivity more than doubled and a large loss was changed into spectacular profits.

His long love affair with philosophy and mysticism sprang from a critical time in America. All his subsequent writing can be seen as being concerned with his lifelong search for purpose and meaning in life; hence it is mostly therapeutic. His journeys to Persia, Turkey and Egypt and the decade of visiting India for three months each winter formed part of this spiritual quest in which he met Sufis, Hindu Holy Men, and Buddhists, both Theravada and Mahayana.

A long term Indophile, he has numerous Indian friends. For many years he supported Tibetans in India by sponsoring young monks.

Foreword

The ideas in this book, if practiced and implemented, can transform your life and the universe you live in. That's a bold statement, but I speak with some authority as I have used the ideas in this book to do just that, and so have many of my students. The concepts enclosed in these pages are simple, but they are so diametrically opposed to the way we are taught and conditioned to think about ourselves and the universe we live in, that it takes practice to realize their results. If you were to invert your thinking as Ted Falconar suggests in this book you would hold the secrets of getting what you want from life.

I first came across Ted Falconar when I was searching for a copy of Alfred Korzybski's *Science and Sanity*. I had been recommended it when I was studying to become a Certified Trainer of Neuro-Linguistic Programming. One of my mentors had read this weighty tome three times! It had to be good. However, it was out of print and I couldn't track a copy down anywhere. Via a series of 'coincidences' I was given Ted's telephone number as someone who might be able to help. He had a copy which he was willing to sell me and he also said that he would send me a copy of the forerunner to this book, *How to use your Nous*. The two books arrived. Korzybski's book running to 800 plus pages and Ted's running to approximately 50! I sat down and read *How to use your Nous* in about an hour. I got real, clear insights into Korzybski's Non-Aristotelian Thinking and a deeper knowledge of linguistics and Neuro-linguistics. I immediately ordered extra copies of the book to sell to my students at my next practitioner training. We sold out on the first day! That was the start of a continual communication between Ted and myself.

If you have studied NLP then take a look at the "Rules for Non-Aristotelian Thinking" in Chapter 1. They'll seem very familiar to you! Also Korzybski's Structural Differential corresponds very strongly with the notion of chunking up and chunking down in NLP. The most powerful realization I got from the book was that words are more than just a means of communication. They are also a means of perception and we structure our universe according to the meanings we apply to words. Words are probably one of the deepest and most unconscious filters we have. I started to realize, when doing therapeutic interventions with clients, that most of us do not use words as they were originally intended and that this, in many cases, was the root cause of what people experience as problems in their life. Words were never intended to have any meaning out of context. Yet most of us would apply multiple meanings to words out of context. As an experiment pick any word at random and ask yourself, 'What does that mean?' Keep asking the same question to the answer you get each time. How many meanings did you get? And the words don't actually mean that at all. Words are meaningless without context.

Words also limit us tremendously. I think everyone has had the experience of attempting to explain to someone how funny an event was and the other person just didn't get it. The comment is usually, "I guess you just had to be there". That's because words are not the experience. They can't be. Have you ever had a most wonderful dream that stayed with you on waking? You really want to share it with someone so you start to put it into words. You struggle at first but as you persist it's almost like the wonder and magic begin to evaporate from the dream until you think, "Oh it wasn't that wonderful after all". The dream you had was a beyond words experience. Pure experience. Words take you away from the experience.

Ted has made Korzybski's original ideas very accessible, blended his own experience of applying them in his life and business, added some quantum theory, and then fleshed them out with his study of Eastern Mysticism. All in a matter of a hundred or so pages. It's quite a combination and quite an achievement.

I hope you get as much from *Creative Intelligence* as my students and I have. As I think about the concepts in the book I am reminded of the visual image of The Hanged Man from the tarot deck. The man is hanging there upside down from a tree yet if you look at his face he looks young, bright and happy. Why? Because he has inverted his thinking from the ways of the world. The path below him is worn, indicating that many have walked this path before. If you too walk the path you will think in a very different way compared to most of those around you. It is, however, a royal path to all of life's riches.

Enjoy!

Dr David Shephard
Certified Master Trainer of Neuro-Linguistic Programming
Director of Research and Training
The Performance Partnership
London
England
www.performancepartnership.com

Note

Nous (Pronounced as in 'house', OED)

I adopted this term as a short word for the use of
Higher Intelligence, which is the basis of Non-Aristotelian
Thinking, i.e. intuition and not verbal rationality. It has also been
used from time to time in the place of Non-Aristotelian Thinking.

The word comes from Greek philosophy's intellectual principle
or Higher Intelligence. It is also familiar in ordinary speech – Use
Your Nous, common sense or gumption; it is used in Western
philosophy for mind or intellect; furthermore it is found in
Gnostic mysticism as the Nous, Angel, Higher Intelligence or
higher being.

I think Korzybski would have approved.

Ted Falconar

Introduction

Alfred Korzybski wrote the large book *Science and Sanity*, which is a work explaining Non-Aristotelian Thinking (Nous). It is a revolution in thinking, which came from his study into the way Albert Einstein thought; his hope was that he could teach ordinary people to think like geniuses.

It also teaches the ancient Eastern idea of Realization. By this word is meant the seeing of reality as it is, and not the commonly held view of the world as made up of hard objects standing out from a solid Earth. This entails seeing through the illusion of words and memory that has been our indoctrination throughout life.

In the East Realization has been taught from the beginnings of human history. The Buddha was the first person recorded as teaching Realization, but he himself learned it from old scriptures – the Vedas and Upanishads of India. Other religions such as Zoroastrianism and Taoism taught it. In Europe the Christian Gnostics taught the same thing; indeed the very word Gnosis (knowledge) implied it. To this day various offshoots of Buddhism, that is Chan, Zen as well as Tibetan Schools, teach it. In India it has been taught throughout the ages and in recent times by such people as Ramana Maharshi, Sri Nisargadatta Maharaj and Krishnamurti.

Though Korzybski seemed to be unaware of Eastern thinking and does not mention it, his teaching in essence is Realization – the seeing of reality.

I think of Nous as the secret of creativity, and creativity as the Elixir of Life, the only one. Throughout my adult life, creativity has been my greatest joy. Everything is transformed by creativity; it is the basis of all human progress. It is vital in strategy just as it is in solving problems and inventing. Without creativity we only exist, but creativity enhances our lives. It is like a magic wand that the creative person has only to wave and it will transform anything into beauty. Without it everything is dull and boring, but as soon as creativity is used the mind gains feelings that are harbingers of ideas and invention. Accompanying these feelings is excitement and pleasure; indeed pleasure, as well as the sense of the beautiful called Hedonic Response or Creative Rapture, is always associated with creativity.

In addition Nous enables us to achieve not only Realization but the associated but higher aim of Eastern philosophy, which is Freedom or Release, called *moksa* in India. Most people are satisfied with materialism; for them the endless proliferation of new distractions will ensure that they remain satisfied. But some people become disillusioned and see the superficiality of materialism. Human beings have always been enslaved. Physical slavery in the old sense is now rare but it has been replaced by subtler chains. Epictetus, the former slave who became a Stoic philosopher, wrote about this in an account of a freed slave who rose to become the friend of Caesar:

> Now he was twice as enslaved as before. He was forever worrying what Caesar was thinking; every gesture and mood of Caesar seemed to be a threat to him. Moreover he knew that if he had to be punished, he couldn't get away with a whipping like a slave. As a great man, a friend of Caesar, he would lose his head.

And that is only one form of slavery – there is a far subtler kind. We human beings think we are masters of words, but in fact they master us: we are word slaves. Nous is the secret of escape from these chains; it is discussed mainly in the last four chapters of this book.

The importance of Non-Aristotelian Thinking cannot be overestimated because it is not only the secret of creativity but of all the highest mental achievements of mankind. It is a fundamental part of poetry, art and invention, but this is not all, for strategy, vision and humour all come from its use; furthermore Non-Aristotelian Thinking means Realization, so the two are linked – a Non-Aristotelian thinker is a Realized being. Yet hardly any effort is made to train human beings in this kind of thinking. Indeed traditional teaching in schools hampers it by inducing a mental block so that children lose the habit of creative thinking and become mere verbalisers.

Krishnamurti and Korzybski had little success in their attempts to teach this kind of thinking because Aristotelian Thinking is entrenched, with practically all teaching posts and positions of power and influence being held by Aristotelian thinkers. More important still is the fact that it is difficult to teach and few teachers of Non-Aristotelian Thinking teach it effectively, so few students ever learn it. As an example Krishnamurti tried to teach Realization, which is the same thing, most of his life, but his followers never learnt it and simply grew old listening to him; in fact I have heard some of them complaining that Krishnamurti led them to a certain point and then left them high and dry. He did not do much more than confuse his followers. Korzybski taught more thoroughly and rationally but he gave little guidance on creativity and never mentioned Eastern methods, which I think can be extremely helpful in learning Non-Aristotelian Thinking. My aim in this book has been to give the essence of Korzybski and also to include these other ways of gaining Realization, which should give the reader the best chance to master Non-Aristotelian Thinking.

The principles of reaching Realization are simple and anyone can understand them verbally; the difficulty is in assimilating them and learning the reflex actions they entail. This is analogous to learning to drive a car where the verbal instruction can be learned quickly but the actual driving requires various subconscious actions which take time and practice to acquire.

This book has been divided into three main sections. The first five chapters give explanation and instruction in Non-Aristotelian Thinking; the second section of five chapters, is to do with its application and use. The last four chapters are about the philosophy of Freedom and Release (*moksa*) of India which can be gained by this kind of thinking, leading to assurance and contentment.

The first chapter goes into Korzybski's Non-Aristotelian Thinking, which came mostly from his book *Science and Sanity*. It is the pith of Korzybski's teaching and it is the rational basis of much of this book.

It is important to bear in mind that Non-Aristotelian Thinking is comparatively easily mastered by a practical adult who is at all creative, and for a young person it is even easier, but verbalisers such as lawyers who spend much of their lives dealing with words will find it more difficult because their semantic blocks are deeply entrenched. I advise those who find any difficulty to read the chapter on Nous quickly and not trouble themselves too much about the precise meaning of every sentence on the first reading; then when they re-read it, they will have gained an overall view and any difficulties should fall into place.

Zen and Tibetan Buddhism have the purpose of teaching Realization, that is, the seeing of reality as it is undistorted by words and memory, precisely what Non-Aristotelian Thinking is about. So their methods are directly relevant to the aims of this book; in consequence I have written a chapter on their ideas. In particular readers should find the Zen Koans and Tibetan meditation helpful to them.

We have to become aware of two entirely different ways of thinking. The verbal one, which most people of the world consider the only way, is uncreative. The other is conducted in visual images, feelings and above all intuitions, which constitute creative thought. In using creative thought we are cut off from verbal memory, which is at the root of our problems, for memory obscures the mind so that we see objects only through a screen of memory; in other words we do not see them as they really are.

Creative thinking occurs in reveries and subconscious thought. It is the same as *buddhi* of Oriental philosophy and *Nous*, the Greek word, used by Plato, Hermes and Plotinus. A chapter goes into the two ways of thinking, which are vital for gaining Realization.

The chapters on Creativity, Poetry and Mysticism have their own importance but they can be thought of as indirect ways of gaining Realization. I mean by indirect that when someone achieves a creative idea, they must have gone through the process of creative thought and it should be possible for them to return to that moment in introspection, and they may suddenly 'see'. Similarly a person who reads a passage of poetry that moves them, or better still who writes it, will be able to analyse their thoughts and return to the state of reverie that is part of creativity.

Creativity can be taught as has been demonstrated by W. J. J. Gordon in his book *Synectics*; further, as he said, it is widespread in the population, indeed it is more likely to be present in the mass of ordinary people than in verbalising intellectuals. It is for these reasons that I think creativity is the best way for most people to gain Realization.

Self-Liberation

The last four chapters in this book are about one of the main aims of existence: Liberation or Freedom, called in India *mukti* or *moksa*. Modern Western ideas about liberation diverged from ancient teachings such as those of Stoics and Indians. Liberal thinkers including John Stuart Mill and Isaiah Berlin made great contributions to the theory of political liberty, but of self-liberation they wrote nothing. Indeed Berlin complained that Epictetus's philosophy was the antithesis of political liberty because it entailed acceptance of tyranny. Berlin himself made the point that political liberty was never absolute, it could never be more than a compromise between the demands of individuals, often mutually conflicting; the needs of the public at large including schooling, children, etc.; and the often baneful ideologies of governments.

The purpose of true liberation, which I have called Self-Liberation, is to make a person free under all circumstances. His only ultimate enemy is himself. To the Stoic or Mystic, nothing outside can ever destroy one's freedom. Compared to the noble words of Socrates and Epictetus and the sublime speech of mystics, the writings on political liberty are Aristotelian and therefore full of abstractions. The first concerns the reality of liberty, the other is mere words about it, which to me are mechanical and robotic, unreal man-made abstractions, and hence ultimately unreal.

Realization is not necessarily a religious idea. A young man at a seminar where my books were available said that *How To Use Your Nous* had transformed his life, just as my life was transformed by Korzybski's *Science and Sanity*. Korzybski's writing is not religious in any way. In fact the highest teachings of Hinduism and Buddhism are about seeing reality; they are rational and scarcely 'religious' in the Western sense. Indeed I have heard some Christians argue that Buddhism is not a religion but a philosophy.*

Realization comes to Buddhists and Hindus in the same way as understanding comes to students of Non-Aristotelian Thinking and breakthroughs to scientists – as a revelation, sudden or gradual. It seems sudden but normally it occurs after a long period of incubation. Kabir the Weaver (born c. 1440) was asked by a disciple when he had become Realized. In a poem he wrote: "I became suddenly revealed in Benares, and Ramananda illumined me; I brought with me the thirst for the Infinite" (Trans. R. Tagore).

Realization and the later Self-Liberation require only a different way of thinking: Nous or Higher Consciousness.

Chapter 8, "The Open and The Shut Mind" goes into the filter mechanism that prevents some people from understanding revolutionary new ideas of which Non-Aristotelian Thinking is one. It also includes the way that this can be overcome by keen perception and use of the Structural Differential of Korzybski.

Koans, the irrational riddles discussed in a chapter of this book, indicate this purpose of Buddhism, which is to blast people out of their ruts of words so they can be freed of the verbal fog that is the mental environment of most people.

Chapter 1
Non-Aristotelian Thinking (Nous)

Not the least of Albert Einstein's achievements was that he thought in an entirely different way from ordinary people. Count Alfred Korzybski studied this and as a result brought out the large work *Science and Sanity*, which explains Non-Aristotelian Thinking. This is an advance in thinking over the Aristotelian comparable to the advance of Einsteinian physics over Newtonian. It is a revolution in thinking and because it conflicts with a lifetime's experience it is difficult for some people to master, though it is in fact quite simple.

Korzybski wrote in *Science and Sanity* (p. 13 & p. 397) that without using the Structural Differential it was very difficult to train people in his system. Below is a simplified Structural Differential to demonstrate the principles; later I shall go into it in more detail. The word "structural" refers to the rule in Nous that the Cosmos is structural, i.e. it has shape, form and pattern. The Structural Differential distinguishes different levels of abstraction and different objects and what is real from what is verbal and illusory. It was his hope that he could teach ordinary people to think like geniuses.

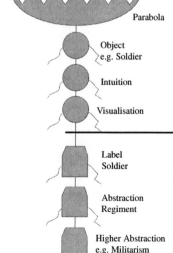

Parabola

Object
e.g. Soldier

Intuition

Visualisation

Label
Soldier

Abstraction
Regiment

Higher Abstraction
e.g. Militarism

The top figure, a parabola, represents the total microscopic and macroscopic characteristics of the object. It is cut off to indicate that it is infinite.

Creative thought: The first circle is an object at the everyday level of use. The second circle is intuition and feeling by which we sense the object.

The third circle is visualisation by which we turn intuitions into visual images. Finally we turn visual images into words.

Korzybski's Unspeakable Level: THE REAL

The Verbal Level: THE NON-REAL

An Aristotelian thinker sees an event or object and recognises it or sees similarities with other objects or events. Instead of looking intently they jump to conclusions and 'think' they know all about the object or event. When such a person enters a garden they do not truly see the flowers, instead they use their memory and see the labels in their mind. They ignore the second and third circles of the Structural Differential and the vital pause needed for thinking.

Worse still, verbal rationality is the subtle chain that binds us. Only by escaping from the verbal level can anyone gain true freedom. These chains are so subtle that hardly anyone is ever aware of them. We are the prisoners of Plato's Cave (see p. 18) who think the shadows are reality.

1

J. Z. Young (1978) pointed out that a person who is blind from birth and then sees as an adult is overwhelmed by the mass of sense impressions, and it takes some time before they are able to recognise anything.

We must think of ourselves as like that blind man. We have chosen from the mass of sense impressions, facades from a limited number of objects that are the familiar world we think is reality, ignoring most of it. So when we look at flowers we recognise them only by the familiar labels in our mind. We do not see the hidden characteristics, what Korzybski called the characteristics left out. As in a marriage, it is these characteristics left out in the original appraisal that can be decisive later. The world before us is not one of hard objects standing out from a solid earth but particles of light striking our retinas, causing bewildering patterns.

To master Non-Aristotelian Thinking it is necessary to be aware of the two modes of thinking. One is the ordinary verbal, analytical and associative method taught in schools; it is memory-dominated and relies on noticing similarities between objects and between events. It identifies objects, giving them names and stating what they are. On seeing something the Aristotelian thinker immediately starts talking about similarities and makes analogies with other objects or events and compares them. This is the habitual method of gossip and prattle; it is always jumping to wrong conclusions.

The other way of thinking, Nous or Non-Aristotelian Thinking, is totally different. The two things that are most important to know about this are, first, that nothing is like anything else – even an electron is unpredictable, two pins are not exactly the same; the other is that our words never cover the object, whatever we say it is, IT IS NOT!

Since nothing is exactly like anything else, it is a waste of time comparing objects. The main effort in Nous is to know the object in its subtlest levels, so Nous looks for differences not similarities. When a Non-Aristotelian thinker sees an object, they remain silent and use intuition and visualisation, not words. They look at events in the same way, seeing their uniqueness, not trying to find analogies or similarities with other events: history does not repeat itself, every episode is unique. Furthermore the search for uniqueness leads to a feeling of freedom because instead of the mind being burdened with all sorts of similarities, analogies and identifications, it is freed just to try to see what really is.

The first of these modes of thinking is uncreative and is a mere shuffling of words and verbal concepts and a ransacking of the brain. The second is creative: it uses very careful perception, then it uses intuition to see into the intricacies of the object or event; finally it feels at subtle levels and then translates the feelings into words.

Korzybski gave a description of scientific discovery, which demonstrates the use of feelings and intuition, on page 22 of *Science and Sanity*: "Creative scientists know very well from observation of themselves, that all creative work starts as 'feeling', 'inclination', 'suspicion', 'hunch', or some other unspeakable affective state, which only at a later date, after a sort of nursing, takes the shape of a verbal expression worked out later in a rationalised, coherent, linguistic scheme called a theorem. In mathematics we have some astonishing examples of intuitively proclaimed theorems, which at a later date, have been proven to be true, although the original proof was false."*

This could refer to all creativity, which is invariably done in the lower centres of the mind, using Nous or Higher Intelligence; in other words using the Unspeakable or non-verbal area of the Structural Differential. A scientist discovers a theory that can be tested; a poet a beautiful idea.

The trouble is that we over-estimate the importance of words and let them dominate us so we lose our grip on reality. It is truly amazing that we should think the noises we make are reality. To use words to sense reality is like going with a lamp to search for darkness.

Worse still, most of us human beings think that we are the masters of words; the truth is they master us, we are enslaved by words.

---

*Korzybski's description of scientific discovery is important. It does not come from words or verbal thinking; it comes rather from intuition and visualisation. To expect to get a creative idea out of verbal thought is comparable to getting a scientific breakthrough by a parrot. Verbal thought comes from the cortex, which is a centre for analysis, not creativity.

There was a brief time when as children we were free. Then we had few words – knowing next to nothing, everything was new to us and we were full of wonder. As we learned more words and our memories expanded, we started to recognise many things, which soon became familiar to us. This familiarity with things leads to boredom, a disease of words. Furthermore we even learnt what things are, which is the grossest ignorance because as Non-Aristotelian Thinking teaches, nothing is what we say it is: everything is unique and unknowable in its subtlest levels.

The mind is our most precious possession but we fill it with harmful thoughts. In his *Journal*, Henry David Thoreau mentioned how we make a very bar-room of our mind's innermost sanctum, as if the dust of the street had occupied our thought's shrine with all its filth and bustle. Instead we should fill it with beneficial thoughts and coloured images. We should make our bodies into a house of pictures, in the words of a mystic. Instead we fill it with words, which make us strangers to ourselves. We are for ever outside talking, when we should be within thinking. This is being at home and it is vital. Above all it lets us know ourselves. "Know Thyself" was the injunction of the Delphic Oracle.

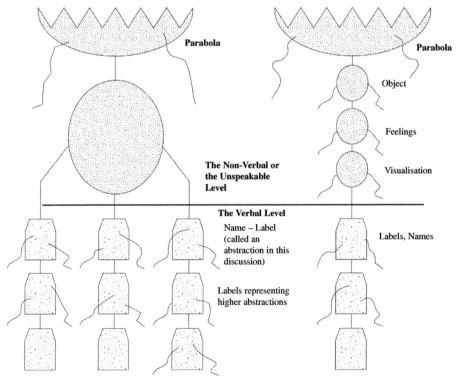

The great Persian mystic poet Jalaluddin Rumi wrote at the start of his major work, the *Mathnawi*, using the image of the reed flute. The reed for making the flute was torn from the reed bed and thenceforth moaned for its homeland. This refers to our own loss of the spiritual world from which we were also torn away. But words have also alienated us from the real world we knew as children. All we must do is release ourselves from the dull classrooms of words into the infinite playing fields of reality.

Above is a more detailed Structural Differential on the left. Let us go over the characteristics again.

The parabola represents the total microscopic and macroscopic characteristics of the object. It is cut off to show that it is infinite. The next figure is the object at the everyday level. Below this are labels: the first row is the name of the object, the next row is a higher abstraction, and the labels below this level represent still higher abstractions; these abstractions can go on ad infinitum. Small circles or dots in the figures represent characteristics that are infinite in the parabola, finite but very numerous in the object at the everyday level and much less in the labels. Strings* hanging loose from the figures represent characteristics of the higher figure not included in the lower, implying that the upper figure is different from the lower. If the large circle is a sheep, the next label would be the name 'sheep', the next label might be 'flock' and the one below a higher abstraction such as 'sheeplike' or 'sheepish', and so on. THE WORD IS NOT THE OBJECT; the object is always far more than the word we give it. The diagram on the right indicates the process of thought.

The parabola and the object are pointed out by teachers of Non-Aristotelian Thinking as being in the Unspeakable Level, meaning that they are beyond words and we can only approach them using keen perception, feelings, intuition and visualisation, not words.

Each vertical set of labels concerns different objects so the lines must be kept apart and must never be confused. Some objects may

---

*Korzybski's original diagram had both loose strings and ones connecting dots of the parabola with the relevant dots of the object (large circle). These make the diagram very complicated and for the purpose of this discussion they are not necessary, so I have left them out.

look like other objects but they are never identical; as I said before, two pins will not be quite the same, indeed even electrons are unpredictable. It is essential to be convinced of this universal truth.

Not only must the vertical sets of symbols be kept apart but the horizontal ones also, because they are at different levels of abstraction and they are never the same.

Rules of Non-Aristotelian Thinking

1. Words are not the things they represent. The words we use about an object never cover the whole object. Whatever we say it is – IT IS NOT!

2. Everything is unique because no two things are ever exactly the same, in other words nothing is identical to something else.

3. Everything must be treated as a whole; the mind, for instance, is not separate from the body. Moreover we are joined to all things at subtle levels. This is a holistic view of the universe.

4. No clear division separates an observer from the object observed; they are linked irrevocably.

5. Reality is structural, not verbal. It has form, pattern and shape.

6. Visualisation is vital to Non-Aristotelian Thinking. It should be thought of as a supremely accurate language for translating reality into the mind.

7. Words give mankind the important ability to pass ideas on from one generation to another and one person to another, but they are limited for they are not near to reality.

8. Nearly all arguments are caused by people confusing different levels of abstraction or by supposing two objects

to be the same when they are different. The Structural Differential is useful for ending such arguments and for seeing through fallacies.

9.   The use of the Structural Differential requires a pause while the mind thinks out a problem; this pause is vital for accurate thinking.

10.   Reality is far from words and it is very different from what a naive person thinks it is; Non-Aristotelian Thinking gets closer to reality, which is an attribute of geniuses and creative people.

11.   The traditional Subject/Object system of logic as seen in the syllogism is fundamentally false and leads to endless confusion. The little word 'all' of the syllogism's "all such and such are" has done more harm to thinking than any other word in language.

12.   An object has many characteristics on different levels such as the macroscopic, microscopic and sub-microscopic. Most of these characteristics are unknown to us so they are not included in the word we give it, the object's name. These characteristics that are left out are decisive and imply that the lower and higher abstractions must never be confused in the same way as the object and its name must not be confused.

13.   The order in which perception should take place is stunted in Aristotelian Thinking, leading to some mental illness. The natural order is to see, pause, feel, sense, intuit, visualise – only later should the mind verbalise. An Aristotelian thinker sees an object and immediately verbalises by noticing some similarity with something else or recognising it – they 'know' all about it.

14.   Many words have multiple meanings so only the whole context of a phrase or sentence is significant.

In the rest of this chapter, I shall amplify these rules.

In the West, education teaches verbal learning, which starts in kindergarten where a word such as 'apple' is spelled out and the child is shown a real apple: the word 'apple' becomes the real apple in their mind, and so our troubles begin. Everyone will see that the word 'apple' is not the real apple; unfortunately this method induces people to behave as if the word is the object. A non-creative intellectual thinks in the same way as children are taught, only their words are longer and more complicated. They enter a world of words, which can be thought of as two-dimensional or even three-dimensional whereas the world outside, reality, is multidimensional.

An analogy for the limitation of words is often found helpful: what goes on in our heads can be likened to a map, and reality to the actual territory the map refers to. However accurate and self-consistent and useful the map, it is still only a map, and the territory with its trees, mountains, rivers and houses is totally different from it.

A child does not start life in this way; they think visually and with feeling just as the jungle savage has to think visually or he would not catch much game. Slowly, as the child's education progresses, they will start to recognise things and know things and it is not long before their childhood is ended and they become bored like many adults. The worst of it is that the brighter the child in the verbal sense, the more likely they are to fall victim to the trap of words and become an intellectual verbaliser of the sort castigated by psychologist Abraham Maslow (1970).

It should not be thought that these people never use Non-Aristotelian Thinking; in such activities as typing, driving a car and cycling, words are almost useless because until the appropriate reflexes are learned by actual trial and error, no one will gain these skills. Moreover, words can be a positive disadvantage. I recall one example of this when I heard two racing drivers giving their views on how to drive round a corner. One of them gave a lucid account of how he did it; the other was almost inarticulate about it, mumbling a few confused words. The first was an ordinary driver, the other the fastest driver of his generation who had little theoretical idea of how he drove round corners, he just did so faster than anyone else.

It is certain that all people make some use of this sub-conscious thinking, but not to a great enough extent. Later in this book it will be shown that we should expand its scope into the actual living of life. The sub-conscious mind is a supreme gift, which Non-Aristotelian Thinking makes use of.

Even in what may seem intellectual occupations where brain work predominates, the intuitive faculty is nearly always decisive. As an example, in running companies, the vital strategic work cannot be done at the verbal and rational level; instead it requires intuition, vision and creative thinking done in reveries and meditation. Furthermore, what is true of a business leader is even more true of a general of an army. In short all creative work, whether it is about strategy, poetry or art, has to be done at the Unspeakable level. Some people voice suspicion of hunches and intuitions but they must learn that this is a higher thinking, which all people should be able to harness.

Use of the Higher Intelligence has nothing to do with the kind of intelligence tested in I.Q. tests. Hans Eysenck (1995) wrote that once a person's I.Q. is about 120 or higher, experience of creative people has shown that other factors are decisive, such as independence of thought and persistence. Conventional intelligence is mainly about memory and associative thinking, which do not lead to new ideas; the other intelligence is about solving problems and creating. Furthermore, because the sub-conscious mind is used, over which the conscious mind has no direct control, it takes a long time for solutions to a difficult problem to come. Examinations and I.Q. tests almost always have a time limit so they cannot test the sort of intelligence needed in inventing and creativity. It is this intuitive intelligence that is decisive in creativity.

The kind of people most likely to understand Non-Aristotelian Thinking are those whose work entails solving problems of the real world and producing creative ideas. Uncreative intellectuals believe that they are nearer to reality than poets and visionaries, whom they speak of as dreamers who write escapist works, but the very opposite is the truth. A look at the Structural Differential will show that the dreamers are thinking in the Unspeakable real and the verbalising intellectuals are entangled in the illusory web of words. Once this becomes clear (and I don't mean an intellectual understanding of it but by conviction of the whole being), it comes as a revelation and it is seen that what we supposed was real is illusion and what we supposed was illusion is real; everything is turned upside down and a sense of freedom is experienced. This is Realization, and when we use Non-Aristotelian Thinking we start to see what actually is. Further, when we use creative thought we become one with reality – then we find a wonderland that is always mysterious and exciting. This can lead on to the heightened states of mystics and poets.

The rule that all things are different is as universal as the law of gravitation. So all objects and events are unique, but verbalising thinkers in looking at reality categorise and identify what they see; to do this they exaggerate similarities and ignore differences and in this manner, instead of looking for uniqueness, they force objects into the categories of their minds.

The practice of categorising and identifying is wrong and infantile. As Korzybski wrote, it is like the logic of North American Indians whose thinking went something like this: all stags run fast, some Red Indians run fast, some Red Indians are stags.

Albert Einstein was able to enter the Unspeakable region without any burden of preconceived ideas and conventional scientific thought so he was able to look at time and space in an entirely new way, whereas his fellow scientists were hampered by their traditional ideas. A creative person can be likened to an explorer of the real world who takes with them the minimum of baggage.

From the beginnings of mankind, languages have taught us to separate things such as mind and body, time and space, outside and inside, which is a very simplistic view – even such things as appear to be separate are really linked irrevocably together. For instance, observer and object observed are linked and this is not just at the quantum level, because it is difficult to say where the stimulus ends and the sense impression begins, for they overlap. It used to be supposed that the universe was a void, and the ether was invented to fill it, but the universe is a plenum, a fullness in which all space is filled with energy in the form of electromagnetic forces, even solid objects being only a denser form of this energy. Thus we are not individuals separated from one another;

rather we are linked and in consequence every action has its effect on other people. As an example, a factory manager is linked to his workers so that if he treats them as second-class citizens, he harms the whole factory including himself.

Even at the material level reality is totally different from what the naive person thinks it is: a pencil has many characteristics that we are not aware of beyond the obvious ones that are useful to us such as hardness of the lead, colour and size. What it is in total is a mystery because it is on three levels: the first is the macroscopic of the everyday experience, then the microscopic and finally the sub-microscopic dance of electrons.

The sub-microscopic electrons have been described as a little like a fan, whose blades can be seen when they are at rest, but when the fan runs they blur and nothing, such as a stick, can pass between them without being struck; in the same way the electrons circle so fast that they have the effect of hardness and only agile rays such as X-rays can penetrate into material.

Not only are human beings taken in by this illusion but there is a double illusion because they impose their habitual ideas on reality, so they do not see accurately. This makes it doubly important for an observer to look very carefully at all objects and remain silent and think at the Unspeakable level of real things.

Unfortunately in human affairs, when Aristotelian thinkers see an event, instead of finding out what is really happening, they decide about it from their own experience, which is likely to be wrong on almost every occasion. The mechanism of this is that when a person is confronted with a problem, they think they have the answer because they see an analogy with some previous event and take action as if the new event was the older event, with disastrous results. Just as no two things are the same, this can be said with equal truth of events: no two events are the same and history does not repeat itself. Work on perception has confirmed that the ordinary mind anticipates events and proceeds by a series of anticipations and confirmations. For instance the sound of a footstep leads to the thought that someone is approaching; the sound of the bell confirms the expectation, and so on. Complicated matters follow the same method with a lot less certainty, so the mind is not open – rather it is conditioned to work within its bounds of experience.

To overcome this automatic way of thinking a pause is vital before the mind comes to a conclusion. To demonstrate the error into which Aristotelian thinkers fall, Korzybski used to make a test at his seminars. Before the class started he would arrange for one of his female students to come to his desk. The class saw him hand her a box of matches, which she 'carelessly' dropped. He immediately became 'angry' and 'abused' her, finally slapping her face. About 90% of students would show their resentment, whereas 10% of them would wait impassively, considering various explanations before making up their minds about what they had seen. The first of these reactions is infantile; the second is adult in which the mind does not impose its ideas on events, instead it tries to make sense of them. The first is vicious, leading to many of our problems and wrong evaluations.

The rule is that before deciding about an event a pause is essential; then after thinking about it and gaining more facts, an opinion may be ventured. Support for this comes from all languages, which have numerous expressions advising a pause before hasty action: "count ten", "hold your horses", "wait a minute" are examples of such advice.*

Korzybski wrote a passage about Smith 1, a man who knows nothing about these discussions. He imposes his ideas on everything; for him there is no Realization of the characteristics left out. He is emotionally convinced that his words cover the object, which includes all the characteristics he is unaware of. He ascribes objectivity and value to words. He thinks of their permanence and definiteness. When he hears something that he dislikes, he does not ask, "What do you mean?" but ascribes his own meaning to the other man's words. Words are overloaded for him as if they had power like the magic words of primitive men. Smith 1 is a dogmatist and he seeks to establish ultimate truths or eternal verities and he is willing to fight for them. Not knowing the characteristics left out, he never recognises that the noises he makes are

---

A further example of this with more application to Nous is the often heard expression "let's sleep on it". This implies giving a difficult problem the benefit not only of second thoughts but of Non-Aristotelian Thinking and meditation, etc.

not the objective realities we deal with. If somebody contradicts him he is much disturbed. Not knowing the characteristics left out, he is always right.

This passage, which I have condensed, shows the cause of many arguments, which are compounded when different cultures and people with different languages meet.

In contrast to Smith 1, a Non-Aristotelian thinker when contradicted will ask, "What do you mean? I do not quite follow you". Two people who sit down to find out what is being said and what level of abstraction is being used will soon end their argument, for few arguments can continue if something concrete is before the arguers and they are looking at it together; arguments are nearly always about verbal confusion, not reality.

In fact Korzybski applied the Structural Differential to the fallacies discussed by Bertrand Russell and Alfred Whitehead in their *Principia Mathematica* (1910–1913) and discovered that it solved fallacies using the simplest rules. By comparison the system of Russell and Whitehead, being Aristotelian, was very complicated and difficult to follow. Most fallacies are caused by confusing different levels of abstraction or by confusing different things, so all that has to be done when using the Structural Differential is to keep the vertical lines apart because they are different things, and the horizontal lines apart because they are on different levels of abstraction. Two examples should suffice to illustrate the method. The perennial sophism of Epimenides the Cretan baffled the ancients. It ran, "when Epimenides the Cretan said 'All Cretans are liars', can we believe his statement?" Russell and Whitehead proved, after long arguments in which concepts of types and illegitimate totalities were applied, that the two statements "Epimenides is a Cretan" and "All Cretans are liars" are both possible and they are not contradictory. Using the Structural Differential even a schoolchild can see that the statement "Epimenides is a Cretan" is on one level and "All Cretans are liars" is a higher abstraction and must not be confused, thus agreeing with Russell and Whitehead.

For another fallacy, let us take the statement that "democracy is the best political system because the majority must be right."

13

Democracy and the majority are different things and must be kept apart; the proof is resting on something that is as much in need of proof as itself.

Reality is ultimately structural in that it has only form and pattern, but it was not structurally that the Ancient Greeks looked at things for they laboured under the delusion that objects such as rocks possessed qualities by which, for example, greyness was attributed to a quality of the rock whereas greyness is a structural characteristic of rocks causing light rays to be absorbed or reflected in particular ways. Even mental activities can be described as patterns of electromagnetic phenomena in the brain. So visualisation is the only 'language' directly in accord with reality, whereas verbal languages are very inaccurate and cannot deal with subtle structures.

In fact Korzybski wrote a passage about structure in science:

> The structural data, however, although they are not particularly emphasised are given in handbooks of physics, colloidal chemistry, bio-physics etc. At present it is realised in science that structure is of extreme importance; but because of identification* it is not realised that structure is THE only possible content of knowledge. This fact of course makes the quest of science uniquely structural. Because of it we come to a very far-reaching general rule, that all understanding, to be such must exhibit or assume structure, thus formulating the supreme aim, and perhaps uniquely indicating the only possible method of science.
>
> (From *Science and Sanity*)

Non-Aristotelian Thinking is not only in accord with structure but it is also in accord with correct human thought processes, whereas Aristotelian Thinking changes the natural order, which can itself lead to mental problems. For instance, Pavlov's experiments with dogs demonstrated that behaviour will worsen if the order of stimuli is altered. The correct and natural order is to look and always be silent, then feel with all the senses; at this point feelings arise and these are translated into visual images and finally into words.

Identification refers to the Aristotelian practice of saying what something is – that is, recognising it instead of looking closely and taking it as unique.

Aristotelian thinkers short-circuit this process by jumping to conclusions without perceiving properly.

Korzybski emphasised the vital importance of translation that changes feelings into visual images and then words, and of the equally vital process of changing words into visual images and feelings. Non-Aristotelian Thinking shows the limitation of words, for they are only a medium between our minds and reality; they have no virtues beyond this limited use. He gave a description of how a book should be 'translated':

> When these higher order abstractions produced by many individuals are absorbed and returned in a modified form to the lower centres as 'Visualization', 'Intuition', 'Feelings', etc., the given individual is closer to the external world than he was before, because he has absorbed, digested and appropriated the nervous results of many more experiences and observations than he himself could have gathered alone. He is able to compare, evaluate and relate, revise and adjust his private experiences and observations with the TRANSLATED experiences from higher abstractions of many more individuals. The translation is indispensable, because the reactions of both levels are entirely different, and comparable only when they are on one level. CREATIVE WORK HAS BEGUN.

The verbal level on which we gossip is for ever separated from the subconscious level on which we live; or put another way, the objective level, which is the real, and the verbal level are separate and can only be bridged by translations of the way of thought of the one into the language of the other. Albert Einstein was aware of this gap between words and reality when he wrote: "As far as the laws of mathematics refer to reality they are not certain; and as far as they are certain, they do not refer to reality."

Nothing that I have written should be taken to mean that intuition or feeling used in Non-Aristotelian Thinking is more accurate than analytical logic; far from it. Einstein himself said that his ideas were wrong 99% of the time. All creative ideas must be tested. This follows the scientific method propounded by Karl Popper, which roughly implies that a scientific statement is one that is capable of being tested. Non-Aristotelian Thinking is all about getting closer to reality so every creative idea must be referred back to reality; not to test creative ideas would be to invite horrific error. Nor should it be supposed that Non-Aristotelian Thinking attempts to do away with rational thinking. Verbal and mathematical logic are vital for getting the intuitions and visions of scientists down into the clear intellectual form and rigour of science. But what must never be forgotten is that these logical and mathematical statements are not reality.

A reader who has difficulty with this chapter should look at Chapter 8 "The Open and The Shut Mind", which discusses the filter or screen mechanism that prevents the mind seeing a revolutionary idea such as Non-Aristotelian Thinking. Here also is Maslow's method of mastering something new and revolutionary, which is of course a clear example of the use of Non-Aristotelian Thinking, in particular its Structural Differential.

I thought the reader of this chapter might find a summary of the main differences between the two ways of thinking of some help:

Aristotelian

This is the naive view of the ordinary person: everything before us is how we have been taught to see it. Each thing has a name and is recognised. We live in a verbal world of the knowing worldly man who knows the price of everything but the value of nothing. It is the dogmatic world of Smith 1.

It is the world of the closed mind. It is memory-dominated. Thought is analytical and associative. The perpetual search is for similarities and comparisons and analogies. Seeing something leads to jumping to conclusions about it, usually wrong.

The memory is used exclusively to solve problems, whereas a truly revolutionary idea cannot be in the memory and its meaning has to be ferreted out. Here there is no creativity, only rationality because only the cortex is used. There are frequent arguments, which are nearly always caused by verbal confusion, not real issues.

Moreover, the natural order of thinking is reversed leading sometimes to pathological illness. The Aristotelian thinker is one of the captives of Plato's Cave, who think the shadows are reality.

It is of direct relevance to Non-Aristotelian Thinking that the philosopher Sir Karl Popper spent a considerable part of his long life attacking what he called Essentialism, that is the obsession of many intellectuals with words and the meaning of words.

This started as a boy of sixteen when he had a hopeless argument with his father and discovered the trap of words. He found himself unable to put across his view of the total irrelevance of arguments concerning words and in contrast the vital importance of arguments about real things and problems, solutions, hypotheses. He gave an analogy for words: the content of letters and their importance in words – is NIL; the content and importance of words in a statement – is also NIL.

He wrote out a permanent rule for himself: "Never let yourself be goaded into taking seriously problems about words and their meanings. What must be taken seriously are questions of fact, and assertions about facts; theories and hypotheses; the problems they solve; and the problems they raise." Much later he added: "This, I think, is the surest path to intellectual perdition: the abandonment of real problems for the sake of verbal problems" (Karl Popper, *Unended Quest*).

Non-Aristotelian

Looking intently without words is of the essence. It is the fresh view of a child. The view is critical, searching. In includes Maslow's ferreting out the inherent truth of something. It is perception-dominated thought, not memory-dominated. The aim is to look for differences not similarities. Above all it is the poet's view of the wonder of reality: nothing is boring here.

Here it is intuition and visualisation that are the primary ways of thinking. The use of pause and silence is vital. Almost as important as the uniqueness of the object is the uniqueness of the moment – the NOW, which is the only reality. It must not be defiled by the past or the future.

17

In living you rely on the Higher Intelligence or Nous. You 'JUST BE!' and in Zen you 'LET GO!' Just as one gives no thought to driving or typing, we give no thought to what we are going to say or do. WE JUST BE! This is FREEDOM.

Plato's Cave

*The captives think the shadows are reality. They are ourselves.
Nous or Non-Aristotelian Thinking teaches how to see reality correctly and even how to see new ideas such as quantum theory; not
by ransacking the memory but by 'ferreting out' the meaning.*

Chapter 2
The Two Ways of Thought

Verbalising and non-verbalising thinking have divided the human race since the first recorded history and it is important to know that they still divide us today. The Buddha and Plato wrote about Realization (the seeing of reality), as did Hermatists in Egypt, Hindus, Gnostics and Buddhists. The creative thinking that is used in non-verbal thinking has been called by various names such as Nous, Higher Intelligence, Intellectual Principle and *buddhi* (from the same root as the Buddha – the Enlightened One in India).

The trouble is that no one has been very successful in teaching non-verbal thinking or its ultimate goal, Realization, because only one or two aspects of it and not all of it has been taught. So the world still thinks in the ordinary way, and it could not be otherwise because without exception schools follow the verbal way – this is even true of schools founded by Krishnamurti, a Theosophist who broke away and started his own movement.

Plato wrote about this illusion of mankind brought about by verbalising thinking:

> And now I will describe in a figure the enlightenment or unenlightenment of our nature: imagine human beings living in an underground cave which is open towards the light; they have been there from childhood, having their necks and legs chained, and can only see into the cave. At a distance there is a fire, and between the fire and the prisoners a raised way, and a low wall is built along the way, like the screen over which marionette-players show their puppets. Behind the wall appear moving figures... of men and animals, wood and stone, and some of the passers-by are talking and others silent. "A strange parable," he said, "and strange captives." They are ourselves, I replied; and they see only the shadows of the images which the fire throws on the wall of the cave; to these they give names, and if we add an echo which returns from the wall, the voices of the passengers will seem to proceed from the shadows.

Suppose now that you suddenly turn them round and make them look, with pain and grief to themselves, at the real images; ...will they not try to get away from the light to something which they are able to behold without blinking? And suppose further, that they are dragged up the steep and rugged ascent into the presence of the sun himself, will not their sight be darkened with the excess of light?

(Plato's *Republic*, trans. Jowett)

Verbalising teaching leads to the production of students with much information but little true knowledge, creativity, insight or intuition; indeed this is the reason why many people who do badly at school often do well in life. They have escaped the chains of conventional thinking and their creative ability is unimpaired. Winston Churchill and Bernard Shaw are well-known examples of failures at school who did well afterwards. Shaw remarked that he left school at sixteen and another year would have ruined him. The number of such people is very large. The inventor Edison had only three months of formal schooling; Faraday educated himself. Abraham Lincoln was largely self-educated. Rider Haggard's school work was so poor that it was thought that he would be unable to make a living in England so he was sent out to Africa. Cecil Rhodes was so ill in England that he had to be sent out to his brother's farm in Africa when he was 17 years of age. Edwin Lutyens, one of the greatest architects of his generation, escaped schooling almost entirely.

In religion, the Higher Intelligence or Nous is vital in all mystic thinking. The great Hindu religious Master Sri Krishna Prem, an Englishman, wrote in his book *The Yoga of the Kathopanishad*, which is an exposition of the Path to Immortality, that aspirants had to understand what he called the two modes of thinking. He wrote:

Thus, when we perceive things as so many separate entities or events, as in scientific studies or in ordinary common-sense, that is the mental (manasic) mode. When on the other hand, we see that –

Nothing in the world is single,
All things by a law divine,
In one another's being mingle
(Shelley, *"Love's Philosophy"*)

the vision, in fact, of the mystic and the poet, we are seeing in the mode of the higher intelligence (buddhi).

If a clear grasp of these two modes of consciring or "seeing" is attained it becomes possible to pick out the elements of lower mind (manas) and higher intelligence (buddhi) respectively in any pattern of experience on any scale whatsoever. Without it we are lost at once.

(Consciring was used as an active form of the passive consciousness.)

The Higher Intelligence is about seeing reality as it is, undistorted by thought and memory; this implies the elimination of prejudice and all preconceptions, in short the contents of memory that act as a screen preventing the mind seeing clearly. This higher way of thinking, which leads to Realization, is gained by using three abilities: accurate and keen perception, visualisation and creative thinking.

After childhood few people ever look at things really carefully. The reader should test this by perceiving an object such as a complicated flower like a delphinium. It must be looked at as if it had never been seen before. In looking at it the eyes should be focused at different distances so that the flower is blurred, and in that process a new insight may be gained and new aspects of the flower may be seen. At the same time the mind should be concentrated between the eyes as if a difficult problem has to be solved. After looking in this way for a long time, the mind will often be surprised by new features that make the flower a unique object; it is this moment that often gives a poet an insight and brings the joy of Creative Rapture, leading to a new way of seeing. An example of this intent looking is given in Chapter 9 "Seeing the Real and the Beautiful" later in this book where I quote the story of a holy man making his new disciple look at a flower day in and day out for many weeks until he learned to see its subtle beauty.

There is nothing really strange in this keen perception because it is the way children think and perceive before they 'know' about things. It is the way we must learn to think habitually. Everything must be looked at just as carefully, so that all landscapes and even the smallest and most insignificant of objects are seen in this way. Not only is this a far more accurate way of seeing but it enables us to transform life into one of interest and joy. When we look at sea or clouds, we should discern a new universe, for all things are not as we think they are; instead they are vibrant and ever changing. In a way it is like looking, as we once did, into the embers of a fire and imagining pictures there, but we are seeing not pictures but reality. In this creative way of perceiving, we do not look for things or 'recognise' things – we are looking for the unique, which is a poet's view; so all words and mental conceptions we have of things must be banished from us.

This same accurate way of seeing will be used by a general of an army or a strategic executive of an industrial company. The seemingly confused scene before them will change in creative thought; they will see with a new clarity and the nub of their problems will become disclosed. Often the solving of a problem is not to do with finding an answer directly but seeing clearly and finding the nub of the problem, and once that is discovered the answer often becomes easy. The search for the problem is a necessary part of scientific discovery, as was shown by Einstein. This will not be found using conventional thinking but it will often appear to the higher creative intelligence.

In his book *Motivation and Personality*, Abraham Maslow wrote a passage that brings out the vital necessity of keen perception:

> The ordinary man stereotypes reality whereas the creative person looks at things for their uniqueness. The scientist of the ordinary sort classifies, labels and explains everything of the world. The artist looks for the unique, he sees things with the freshness of the child.

> Every psychologist knows that it is possible for a person to live by a set of ready made ideas that were acquired complete in the first decade of his life and will never be changed. Such a man may have a high I.Q. He may therefore spend time in intellectual activity, selecting lists of evidence that support his ready made ideas, but this is not creativity or productive thinking. His problem is blindness to the real world, imperviousness to new evidence, distortion in perceiving and remembering; and above all a mind that has ceased to develop. And further: Creative thinking is allied to the perceptual process not the memory process. The main

part of creative thought is in perceiving as clearly as possible the intrinsic nature of a problem. It is examined in its own right, in its own style, almost as if no other problem existed. The main effort must be in ferreting out its own intrinsic nature. In contrast in associative thinking it is rather to see how the problem resembles other problems previously experienced. Of these two methods, the first or holistic-dynamic, if it has any meaning at all, has the meaning of creativeness, uniqueness, ingenuity and inventiveness. Thinking is the method by which mankind creates something new, which in turn means it must be revolutionary in the sense of conflicting with what is already known. If we were permitted a slight exaggeration, thinking might be defined as the ability to break our habits and to disregard our previous experience ... Creative thinking requires boldness, daring and courage. Education of the conventional sort makes no effort to get the individual to examine reality directly and freshly; rather it gives him a pair of prefabricated spectacles with which to see the world conventionally; what to like, what to approve, and what to feel guilty about.

(Maslow's passages from *Motivation and Personality* have been compressed.)

Visualisation is nothing less than inner sight, which to a mystic is more valuable than outer sight; so much so that some wise men have blinded themselves to 'see' better. Democritus was voluntarily blind yet it was said that he saw more than the rest of Greece.

Visualisation furnishes the bare walls of the mind, the soul's stark rooms with pictures. To visualise is to break out from a black and white landscape into a landscape of flowers, birds and butterflies. More than this, it is the only way to see the microscopic levels of reality. The blunt instruments of words are replaced by hieroglyphs of complex numbers, but even these fall short of describing the micropictures of quantum reality. I imagined a visualisation of this sub-world of coloured pictures:

Quantum Light World

In the mind are fields of poppies.
When I enter, I breathe the opium
That carries me into a world
That lies between the moments.

23

> Here time is slowed and the light
> Is frayed to pure strands of colour.
>
> I cast my hands over my eyes
> For the colours burn like fire.
> Here photons spread their bright wings
> These micro-butterflies of the spectrum,
> And fly like fireflies flashing
> Through forests of burning light.

Visualisation is in accord with reality and it can be thought of as a language, the universal language of the Cosmos. In spite of its virtues, visualisation is not part of the training in schools; in fact verbalising training harms it so that some people leave school having practically lost the ability to visualise. The vital necessity for visualisation in most creativity is clear; it is also part of vision and of all the highest activities of the mind. One of its principal tasks is to translate the feelings and intuitions of Higher Intelligence into visual images, which can then be translated into words or mathematical symbols; it is also used in the reverse process of changing words into visual images and then into the original feelings of the poet or mystic who wrote the words.

Fortunately for those who have lost the ability to visualise, visual and verbal thinkers are not completely differentiated: no one is completely visual or completely verbal, so that training to re-acquire visual thought is not as difficult as it might have been if there had been no visual experience at all. In fact it is only necessary to do some practice in which different shapes are brought before the mind. At first they should be rudimentary figures such as squares and circles, but later complicated figures should be used and in different colours until the mind is able to reproduce all objects of the outer world. In Yoga such instruction is called Antara Yoga, which can lead on to a disciple developing what is called telescopic sight. To master visualisation is to gain a supreme gift.

Creative thinking is completely different from ordinary thinking in which an object is seen so that its sense impressions come to the eyes; the two, the thinker and the object of thought, remain separate. But in creative thought the two become one; this is done by visualisation and feelings so that the thought seems to envelop the object and become part of it. This will become clear only by personal experience: the description of the method used in this kind of thinking will vary from one person to another, but for some the brows may be slightly furrowed as thought is concentrated between the eyes. In this process the thoughts seem to be projected round the object and they interpenetrate it. The word *dharani* that I have used for introspection in paragraphs on Tibetan meditation comes to mind. In this seeing the mind visualises and feels the object without verbal thought and a new aspect of the object comes to the mind after long and intent thinking. A similar way of thinking has been described in books where patients are taught to visualise their illnesses and imagine the beneficial effect of medicine on the part that is diseased; to do any good, visualisations and feelings in which the mind seems to penetrate the ill part are essential, whereas ordinary shallow visualisation would be useless.

Using this deeper kind of visualisation and feeling, an insight may come suddenly and at a moment when it is least expected. I was often posed problems at my office when I was Managing Director of a company; I rarely tried to find a solution then, but later in the evening or in the midnight hours when I was alone, I would meditate in the way I have just described and solutions would often come to me.

The need to avoid memory and recognition is vital. Non-Aristotelian Thinking was used by Albert Einstein, who entered the Unspeakable without any preconceived ideas. His had to be a total revolution in science. He used the Tensor Calculus to eliminate all anthropomorphic ideas from his calculations. The value of the Tensor Calculus for this purpose was described by E. T. Bell: "the calculus threshes out the laws of nature, separating the observer's eccentricities from what is independent of him with the superb efficiency of a modern harvester" (quoted in *Science and Sanity*, p. 571).

Einstein's Theory of Relativity came out of the problems he faced in that the old laws of physics were at variance with some observed facts. To solve these difficulties required a radically different way of thinking in which previously held ideas had to be swept aside and what seem to be amazing paradoxes had to replace them. Warped space, ideas of space and time being linked, and the amazing idea that the speed of light does not vary with the speed of the observer relative to it, were some of the new ideas replacing the old.

Chapter 3
Krishnamurti

The following is typical of numerous talks I listened to at Madras (now Chennai), South India. At exactly six o'clock in the evening, just as the sun was setting, Krishnamurti would mount the dais and speak. These talks were given in the genial warmth of January. The atmosphere of a large crowd in a fine garden was conducive to philosophical thought.

He spoke conversationally and not as a lecturer. As he kept repeating, he and his audience were having a discussion about certain matters of common interest into which they were making enquiries; he was not, he said, a lecturer. I have condensed his rambling style:

> Human beings are in a state of conflict. The human brain has been conditioned by 50,000 years of thinking that conflict is mankind's natural state. Health is affected because these conflicts cause psychosomatic illness and dissatisfactions. And they affect energy, which hampers anyone who is in a state of conflict, but if the being can see things without conditioning it leads to great energy and enthusiasm.
>
> Why do human beings, who have such intelligence, have this problem?
>
> The reason is that the brain is taken up in the problem; if there were only problems and a brain that had no problems, then it would be easy.
>
> Is it possible to live without problems? Because the brain accepts problems as part of existence, it is itself the main problem. Politicians have many problems and they try to solve them with brains that are muddled with problems and so they cause even greater problems.
>
> Problems are a challenge. Since childhood we have had challenges thrown at us – we must learn maths, we must achieve this and that. And religion does not help. The

Christian is conditioned to have faith, the Buddhist is taught to have the exact opposite. We become so tired of problems that we cease to think, and look to people like the speaker to solve the problems for us.

Time is one of the vital factors because instead of living in the now, we live partly in the past and partly in the future. It is not of the present in which all existence lies. Freedom is destroyed by the illusion of time; the concepts of the past, the present and the future are erroneous, and only when we can live in the moment can we escape into freedom.

Becoming something, ambition and desire are all enemies of freedom because they imply dissatisfaction with the present, which is the whole of reality. It is only possible to have a brain without problems if we understand time. Time past, future and present is all held in the now. It is very important to know that time is in the now. Inquire into time, the now is in the future, can you understand this?

Every problem must be solved beyond time, instantly. That implies perception of the problem, not according to judgement, opinion, etc., but with your whole being in it. When time becomes important, the problem can be seen profoundly, then no problem arises for the brain.

If you approach a problem with a solution, that is no answer, but if you approach it without bias, without anxiety and with vitality and strength, then problems end. Then the brain escapes from its linguistic chains, that is, it gets real freedom. Is this too intellectual? No, it's commonsense.

The word is not the object. When words are used without emotion they are chains, but if there is true emotion then we can be free. We cannot escape from the chains of words and rationality because words are limited. When the brain escapes from its linguistic chains it becomes extraordinarily active and not dissipated. Then you can look at a problem and understand it, for all these things dovetail into one another, they are one movement.

You can't start with a clean sheet, the mind has recorded everything. Conflict makes the mind dull. The brain must be kept in good condition, it must be oiled. There is in the mind, the entity and the analyser; what you must do is look at things without analysing. It is like a map and you see all the countries of the world.

Fear is not an object; the word "fear" is a moment in time. There is psychological time – I will be wise one day whereas I am ignorant now. I live now, I will die; I have a job but I may lose it. Most people fear in this way. There is a record of fear in the brain, knowledge is fear. It becomes fear, the word "fear" contributes to fear.

You insult me or flatter me, it does not record. The kind of knowledge I have to write is harmless but psychologising knowledge is recorded.

Do you ever see the beauty of the sunset? You are too preoccupied with your self. The word "tree" interferes so that you do not see the tree, it acts as a barrier. Do you ever really look with all your senses? Sky, trees, and then in that observation there is no self.

What has to be realised (and Krishnamurti does not explain it very well, but Korzybski does), is that verbal thinking is deadly, because it comes from memory and never solves a problem. The only way fear can be beaten is by non-verbal thinking, which looks at things in a new way. The two ways of thinking work together so that creative thought can be checked by analytical thought, but analytical thought on its own can never solve anything because it is barren.

The points made by Krishnamurti refer to verbalising thinking, which is the way taught in schools; it has conditioned the mind for 50,000 years of human experience. It is a way that never solves problems but is always preoccupied with them, which is why many people suffer fear and anxiety. When a problem is studied really deeply and creatively using visualisation and feelings so that it is seen in its subtlest depths, memory is cut off and anxiety and confusion cease. In that instant the problem and the solver of the problem become one and even the illusion of time ends.

Neuroses, mental distress and psychological fears come from sterile verbal thinking, whereas their solution can come only from creative thinking. Ordinary verbal thinking contributes greatly to the problem, leading to neuroses and multiplying the mental distress and fears.

Krishnamurti emphasised the need to look at the object or problem with the utmost attention as if it had never been seen before, which is a salient rule of Non-Aristotelian Thinking. To see a sunset as Krishnamurti suggested, we have to use creative thinking and feel and sense it with new eyes. Here is a description of a sunset by Thoreau, who was a thinker like Krishnamurti and observed nature in the way we all should – with intensity and creative insight:

> I go forth each afternoon and look into the West a quarter of an hour before sunset, with fresh curiosity, to see what new picture will be painted there, what new panorama exhibited, what new dissolving views. … Every day a new picture is painted and framed, held up for half an hour, in such lights, as the Great Artist chooses, and then withdrawn, and the curtain falls. And then the sun goes down, and long the afterglow gives light. And then the damask curtains glow along the western window. And now the first star is lit, and I go home.
>
> (Thoreau, *Journal*, Jan. 8, 1852)

This is prose-poetry and it gives a description of how we should habitually think. This should not be very difficult because it is the way we all thought as children. It is often pointed out that a child is full of wonder, but as soon as they begin to *know* all wonder in life departs and boredom sets in. It is easy to see why: when the person is a child, they perceive intently, looking at everything freshly because they recognise nothing. Later this keen perception ends and they start to look at things cursorily, recognising them or noticing similarities and analogies with other things. Their interest in life is at an end and their childhood is over.

I myself attended a number of Krishnamurti's talks and read several of his books, but I have to confess that I gained only a vague idea of what he was trying to teach, though I found his writing very poetic. It was not until I read Korzybski's *Science and Sanity* and above all reached the chapter on the Structural Differential that everything fell into place. From that time on Krishnamurti's talks became transparent for me.

Chapter 4
Zen Koans and Tibetan Meditation

The main purpose of Zen and a part of Tibetan Buddhism is to teach how to see reality. In Zen riddles called koans are used upon which a student will spend many hours of thought. It is necessary at the outset to know that there is no rational explanation of koans; their purpose is to jolt the students out of their habitual reliance on verbal rationality and bring them into the real world. So it is pointless trying to understand koans in the ordinary rational way.

The first koan was used by the Buddha. When asked what reality was, he simply raised a rose over his head and smiled at his leading disciple. The rose is forever beyond words, it is in the Unspeakable of Korzybski's Non-Aristotelian Thinking. It has to be sensed by the five senses and not talked about.

An example of a more modern koan is one in which the teacher asks a student how a goose might be removed from inside a glass bottle. The student makes a gesture of pouring the contents out of the bottle and says, "There it is out!"

A more elaborate koan is one called the Sound of the One Hand:

> The Master asked: "In clapping both hands a sound is heard; what is the sound of one hand?"
>
> Answer: The pupil faces the Master, strikes a posture and without a word thrusts one hand forward.
>
> Master: "If you have heard the sound of one hand, prove it."
>
> Without a word the pupil thrusts one hand forward.
>
> Master: "It is said that if you hear the sound of one hand, one becomes a Buddha."

> Without a word the pupil thrusts one hand forward.
>
> Master: "After you become ashes, how will you hear it?"
>
> Without a word the pupil thrusts one hand forward.
>
> Later the Master says: "The Mount Fuji-summit-one-hand, what is it like?"
>
> The pupil, shading his eyes with one hand, takes up the pose of looking down from the summit of Mount Fuji and says, "What a splendid view!"
>
> Master: "Attach a quote to the Mount Fuji-summit-one-hand."
>
> Answer: "Floating clouds connected the sea and mountain. And white plains spread into the states of Sei and Jo."

The whole thing is logically meaningless. You have to get away from everyday rational thought and just BE.

Although Non-Aristotelian Thinking is at the root of a koan, the student goes into a state of crisis; it is at this point that ordinary consciousness is about to "tip over" in D. T. Suzuki's phrase, into the Unknown, the Beyond, the Unconscious. This crisis, when successfully resolved, ends in *satori* (awakening, Realization); as Suzuki wrote: "All Koans are the utterances of Satori with no intellectual mediation; hence their uncouthness and incomprehensibility."

Some people think of the Zen world as being strange. As an example Yoel Hoffmann, who wrote the book he called *The Sound of the One Hand*, had this to say about it:

> Now, at the beginning, I ask you to remember that the world you are entering is odd to almost everyone, even to those who have lived in it for a long time. It multiplies paradoxes; and yet its oddness like the paradoxical oddness, of a dream, verges on the familiar. Odd and familiar as a dream, Zen is meant, however, to occupy the daylight, by means of an irrational reversal of the quality of our lives. For Zen says that we are self-deceived, split and unhappy.

In fact I take issue with Hoffmann. Most enlightened people say this world after enlightenment is not different. Before it was seen through the haze of memory and words, now it is seen as it is; in fact the way we saw it as children. It is not a strange world at all, it is only that we have not been seeing it correctly. As soon as we stop verbalising and start intuitive thinking the world takes on what at first seems an odd appearance, but soon it becomes familiar. We see not an irrational world but a far more rational one, and in seeing the Unspeakable, which Zen calls SUCHNESS or AS-IT-ISNESS, we find the really real.

Tibetan Meditation

I attended a dozen lectures by Professor Samdhong Rimpoche, Principal of the Centre for Higher Tibetan Studies at Sarnath, Benares. Seven of these lectures were about meditation, whose whole purpose, he said, was how to see reality. What struck me at once was the clinical precision of the method leading to the one aim: HOW TO SEE REALITY AS IT IS, undistorted by thought.

As with Krishnamurti's method, Tibetan meditation is designed to stop the mind being confused by innumerable thoughts that come into it in ordinary thinking. He used the expression "scattered thought" for this; as soon as the meditator loses concentration, their thoughts scatter.

He started by saying that preparation is needed before meditation even starts, the first necessity being right purpose. Some people want to feel good or they want to to overcome sleeplessness and other conditions. But the purpose must be to see reality, though many of these conditions are helped by meditation. The meditator must find a quiet place that is not too cold nor too hot, where they will not be disturbed. Preparation will have to include discussion of the amount of time that the aspirant will have to give to meditation. The Rimpoche said that long ago monks meditated for up to two hours at a stretch, but now they do only thirty minutes to an hour at one sitting. Squatting, which includes the half-lotus position, is difficult for Westerners because the pain after about thirty minutes is distracting, and it is not necessary; sitting in a chair is satisfactory provided the meditator's back is straight.

Lying down is not recommended because of the likelihood of the meditator falling asleep.

One or two sessions a day is enough, and if feelings of sinking or any other unusual discomforts occur, the meditation should be broken off and a start made another day.

Sometimes meditation becomes so unsatisfactory that it should be abandoned for several days or even a week and more before making a new start.

The mind must be in a state of calm; this is achieved by the practice of slowing the breath, which has a steadying influence on the mind. Next a suitable object, which is light in colour, has to be chosen as the subject of meditation. It can be a flower or, as the Rimpoche suggested, a golden Buddha or any other object. If after using it for some meditative sessions the thoughts still move erratically, another object should be chosen until one that is effective is found. The colour and size of the object must be congenial to the meditator but it must not be larger than a human being nor so small that it is difficult to see. The height of the object in relation to the meditator must next be decided upon; some people prefer it to be above them and some below, but it must be at a height so that in looking at it, the head does not have to be moved. Before meditation starts, the object must be looked at closely and then the eyes must be shut when an image of the object will appear in the mind; it is this image, not the actual object, that must be meditated upon.

When meditating the eyes should be slightly open; if the meditator finds difficulty when the eyes are open, the room should be darkened.

The meditator sometimes gains certain pleasures but these must be rejected as of little importance compared to gaining Realization.

The meditator is learning to see what really is; there must be no distortion, the mind being absolutely clear, absolutely attentive and focused. After some time the mind becomes absorbed in the image, this state being called *dharani*; later still the mind may reach *samath* (tranquillisation) and finally *samadhi*. This last state is "earnest contemplation", according to D. T. Suzuki; another word for it is absorption.

The word 'transcendent' is used of the Unspeakable region where objects are seen beyond the gross senses. When Samdhong Rimpoche was asked what the transcendent was he answered: "The transcendent is when the thought, the observer and the object become one." They never become one in ordinary verbal thought, for words act as a screen obscuring reality and separating the I from all that is round it. But with visualisation and feeling they do become one; anyone who thinks about this will be convinced of the fact. This is part of seeing reality, because when the observer, the thought and the object coalesce, the separation that is called dualism ends and the being becomes part of reality.

Korzybski emphasised external perception and visualisation; nonetheless they both teach the same seeing of reality as it is in the Unspeakable. No method, however, is very successful at teaching realization, hence my advice to try all methods until you reach one that is effective for you. Samdhong Rimpoche said with humility that he had helped hardly anyone to realization in his years of teaching.

The reader will have noticed that there is a large difference in the way of teaching in the West and the East. In the East it is more to do with actual experience and practice, whereas in the West it is more verbal. A Japanese Tea Master, whose methods have come from Zen, told me that in the West people always ask "Why?" whereas the Eastern person asks "How?" Teaching realization by words alone is like teaching a game of skill from a book. It may seem that realization might not fit in the same category but it does. No doubt some verbal instruction helps at the outset but once that has been absorbed, the aspirant must do it himself by meditation and introspection. The whole thing in Buddhism is to do it yourself. The Buddha's oft quoted words were: "Work out your own salvation with diligence." Teachers can only point out vaguely the right direction that must be followed.

Let us not forget that in the West the vital need for intuition in creativity has only recently been advocated (H. Eysenck, *Genius*, 1996). We can learn much about intuition and Realization, especially the training, from sages who were teaching this way of thinking 2,500 years ago when the people of Europe were mostly painted savages.

Chapter 5
Meditation, the Seeing of Reality

People in the West think of meditation as a practice that is done only occasionally, in which objects such as flowers or a candle flame are thought about; they may also have heard of mandalas, which are subjects of meditation in religions. In fact meditation is about the second or Nous mode of thinking as discussed earlier in this book, and it should be practised habitually and all life long. Meditation is the clearing out of the mind so that it can see without distortion brought about by our schooling and memory. Meditation is also about happiness, which comes from cheerful and beneficial thoughts.

Unfortunately we fill our minds instead with worthless information and allow ourselves to be assailed daily with harmful news. Henry David Thoreau (1817–62) in America complained about this in his generation, and ours must be incomparably worse:

> Think of admitting the details of a single case of the criminal court into the mind, to stalk through its very sanctum sanctorum for an hour, aye, many hours! To make a very bar-room of your mind's innermost apartment, as if for the moment the dust of the street had occupied your very mind of minds, your thoughts' shrine, with all its filth and bustle! Would it not be an intellectual suicide?
>
> *(Journal)*

Meditation not only can give happiness because it is the basis of Non-Aristotelian Thinking and hence creativity, it also gives a deep compensation for disappointments and tragedies of life. The Stoic Seneca in his incomparable consolatory letters to his friend Lucilius wrote: "Success comes to the common man, and even commonplace ability; but to triumph over the calamities of mortal life is the part of a great man only. Truly, to be always happy and to pass through life without a mental pang is to be ignorant of one half of nature." He added, "The Gods desire above all things to see great men struggling with adversity." But there is even more gain in misfortune than philosophers have proclaimed. All things that we met with in life and thought of as disadvantages in the beginning are found to be helpful in the end; and all those things that in youth we thought were advantages come to be seen in the end as harmful. There is an inherent justice in life, which takes the form of a deep compensation that causes the senses of those who have suffered to become more acute so they discern a subtler beauty. Homer and Milton were blind and Beethoven deaf. The philosopher Seneca lived under the tyranny of the mad Emperor Nero, his advice for some years ameliorating the lot of the Romans, but eventually he was ordered to kill himself. Tchaikovski was also ordered to kill himself; I have always thought of his Pathétique Symphony as being the compensation for his tragic death. Tragedy is the terrible spur for sublime works of beauty.

Thoreau lived a lonely but joyful life in which he meditated creatively. He was far from religious in the conventional sense yet he thought like a mystic and this is manifest in all his writings:

> In the street and in society I am almost invariably cheap and dissipated, my life is unspeakably mean. No amount of gold or respectability would in the least redeem it, dining with the Governor or a Member of Congress!! But alone in distant woods or fields, in unpretending sproutlands or pastures tracked by rabbits, even in a bleak and, to most, cheerless day like this, when a villager would be thinking of his inn, I come to myself. I once more feel myself grandly related, and that cold and solitude are friends of mine. I suppose that this value, in my case, is equivalent to what others get by church-going and prayer. —This stillness, solitude, wildness of nature is a kind of thorough-wort, or boneset, to my intellect. This is what I go out to seek. It is as if I always met in those places some grand, immortal, infinitely encouraging, though invisible companion, and walked with him.
>
> (*Journal*, Jan. 1857)

Meditation brings the mind into a state in which it can intuit, sense, visualise, enter reveries and daydreams, all of which are used in Nous. The mind escapes from its chains of memory and words, which prevent it seeing reality. When we are in a garden, we must truly 'see' flowers beyond the mental labels, which allow us to see only the dead flowers of our minds.

The one vital necessity in meditation is relaxation. In fact relaxation is the most important skill to master for other reasons, not the least of these being its usefulness in combating tension, which is a bane of health. For a novice in the art of relaxation, it is necessary to start by relaxing the extremities of the body and then gradually progressing through all muscles, first tensing and then relaxing them. This will take a few minutes, but for someone proficient in relaxation it can be done quickly and they can move on to the last two, the eyes and the mind. The eyes are focused at a little distance on an object and then relaxed; this is repeated several times until the signs of full relaxation are felt. Finally the mind is made to imagine a clear, bright image, which is allowed to fade; after repeating this several times, numbness, which is often associated with total relaxation, will be felt.

The mind is now in the Nous mode of thought, which is suitable for solving problems and creating. What is being used is the entire intelligence, not just the narrow band of intellectual and rational intelligence we usually rely on. Ideas, images and thoughts come to the blank screen of the mind. This process is analogous to the way a radio or TV set tunes into the airwaves. After practice this mode of thought can be entered into rapidly and at will; it is the way we should spend most of our thinking life.

At his talks worldwide, Krishnamurti taught about seeing reality as it is and not the verbal illusion most people mistake for reality. He used to say that the whole of life should become a meditation in which the real is seen.

Meditation is also about awareness, which is totally different from consciousness, the usual thinking that goes on in the waking state. Awareness is standing back from these thoughts, indeed from the whole process of thought, and just witnessing what is going on. Awareness is about seeing reality. It contrasts with the popular idea of awareness, which is to do with keeping track of material objects and events and our shallow streams of thoughts. A story was told of the inventor Edison when he was in a Post Office. After standing in line for some time, he reached the front of the queue but could not recall his name so he had to retreat to the back to recollect it. Some people would say that he was unaware, but he was probably more aware than the ordinary uncreative person who seems to be aware of everything except what is important.

Awareness is about forgetting, deliberate forgetting, especially forgetting oneself.

Meditation is about changing from the ordinary verbal, rational mode of thinking to the visual, perceptive, intuitional way that is the Nous mode. This is to leave the narrow material plane for the universal. The pleasure of this meditation may fall short of the sheer joy of Creative Rapture and the Peak Experience when creating or discerning beauty but it is more lasting, calmer and one of the truest benefits of the human race. I can think of hardly anything in the world that I would rather do. All other pleasures sate or cloy, but this is lasting and will be a sanctuary, a haven throughout life; in fact in old age it especially blossoms.

Meditation is also about happiness in that we are what our thoughts make us, so cultivating beneficial thoughts is meditation. No one who has learned to meditate in the silence of the soul and found joy in it can ever feel loneliness, for this is a discourse with the whole Cosmos. It is possible to meditate and in a few moments enter states of rapture.

Words are the main obstacle on the spiritual path, which can be seen in pure intellectuals, people whose lives are dominated by words. In Arabic they were called the Mutukallimun, people of words, who were complained about by Ibnal-Arabi and other mystics; verbalisers who would never be able to comprehend realization. Their whole life is of words, so they become alienated from reality. We should be on our guard against this because to some extent we are all slaves of words and we are constantly assailed by them; moreover, even our internal thoughts are mainly in words. Meditation can help to break this damaging habit, allowing the being to escape from the chains of words that enslave them.

This is one of the purposes of seers when they practise silence, refusing to speak for long periods. Silence and wordlessness derail the trains of words that otherwise continually run on the railway lines of the mind. Instead visualisation and intuitive thought replace words. Words are pedestrian and earthbound, whereas with visualisation our thoughts take wing and enter the transcendent. Visualisation can paint the mind with many pictures and take us beyond time and space to the world of 'Here Now'.

Chapter 6
Self-Fulfilment
and Higher Human Needs:
Creativity and Success in Enterprise

One of the most important aspects of Nous is its ability to fulfil higher human needs. Abraham Maslow, whose theories have been applied with much success by some companies, taught the hierarchy of human needs; these in ascending order (starting with the most basic) are: warmth and shelter; food; safety; feelings of belonging; love from someone, e.g. mother; self-esteem; esteem of colleagues; achievement of creativity; the Peak Experience and the desire for the beautiful.

Once a need is fulfilled the being moves to a higher need and the previous one no longer frustrates or motivates. A need that is not fulfilled leads to frustration and ultimately neurotic behaviour. In contrast, a need that is fulfilled leads to psychological growth, improved health and happiness. Some people are unable to fulfil all their needs but sublimate them by philosophy and religion. Others are satisfied with life at a relatively basic level – a few beers with friends and a full stomach are enough for them. Still others are satisfied by non-motivational rewards such as plush offices, large company cars, etc. These people are not motivated by achievement and success. Finally there are some for whom success is everything and they scorn big offices and cars; these make the best managers and executives.

One of the main causes of dissatisfaction in industry is the frustrating of human needs. When a management is harsh and treats employees with contempt and fails to provide work where initiative and success are possible, then it must expect anti-social behaviour. These needs are so powerful that the workers cannot stop themselves. But if management uses these needs to harness the abilities and energy of employees, astonishing success is possible.

Managers must believe that nearly all employees are fundamentally reliable and seek responsibility; in their own homes they are entirely reliable. Lower workers, when given responsibility, almost always rise to it with enthusiasm and do a superior job. This can release higher employees to do more challenging work; finally it can allow managers and executives to cease supervision and 'putting out fires' and get on with the true executive functions of thinking, long-range planning, strategy, and so on. In this way the whole organisation can be upgraded.

In such an organisation it will be found that problems get solved quickly and employees become more effective and cohesive throughout the organisation.

At first management has to gain the confidence of employees by treatment that is supportive and genuinely friendly; it must demonstrate integrity. Once this confidence is gained, and not before, incentives can be applied.

What can be achieved by a really motivated organisation is found hard to believe by a traditional management. Lincoln Electric Company of Cleveland, Ohio, applied such methods. Its employees produced four times as much output as rival companies. Here supervision was irrelevant – when all employees are striving for their fellow workers what would a supervisor do? Real discipline does not come from threats or punishment by management but from informal pressure of fellow workers.

For a short time a pressurising management can do better than a supportive one, but after about a year countervailing forces are created so that performance drops catastrophically. A manager might bear in mind a statement by Maslow from a purely humanitarian standpoint: "Anyone who is harsh, unkindly, contemptuous is a force for mental illness; and anyone who is kind, considerate, helpful is a force for mental health."

An extremely generous suggestion system can harness the entire creativity of a company and at the same time ensure that it is an exciting and stimulating place to work in. Lincoln Electric Co. gave employees the entire proceeds of any suggestion of an employee; Lincoln Electric gained only the overheads. This generosity can be contrasted with the niggardly 10% of the first two years' saving, which is often the formula of companies for successful suggestions.

A manager should not stand back and just supervise subordinates in the old overseer way. A manager should be a guide and mentor. What has to be done is to show the subordinate what they have to do to succeed, give them every encouragement and support, apply goals and incentives to stretch them; and when they succeed, commend them, reward them, promote them. Then success is almost inevitable. The really successful executive gains much of their satisfaction from seeing the young people they have chosen and nurtured become successful; their success is almost the executive's greatest success.

Ultimately the real worth of a company must be measured in the motivation, brains, skill and above all the creativity of its employees.

Success should be the yardstick for almost everything in a company. For instance a top executive is thought by some people to need a long list of qualifications; so many in fact that it makes you wonder if even a universal genius could fill the post. In truth all that they have to do is succeed. This clears away a load of useless debris. When everyone in a company is aware that success alone is necessary for promotion and rewards, it focuses the entire energy, which can otherwise be frittered away in irrelevant sidelines that have next to nothing to do with the vital aims of a company. In the selection of candidates for promotion this makes the process not only fair but easy. The person who did best wins; to the failures it is only necessary to say that so-and-so did better. If at another opening you do better then you will be given the post. This is not only the fairest way but it has its own built-in spur.

To make this yardstick of success crystal clear, it is a good idea to try to make every post a profit centre, meaning that success is clear and not based on judgement and subjective opinion. This also implies that supervision of the old overseer type is not needed; the job of the boss is to lay down the budgeted targets, which will be seen to be exceeded in due course. In fact workers should have control over their area of responsibility without others peering over their shoulders. Everything should be clear without any fuzzy areas where workers are not sure if something is their responsibility or that of the boss, which can lead to horrendous errors and, worse still, uncertainty and its accompanying fears.

A strategy-based company will use their long-range plan to form the one-year plans that are the blueprints for the operating divisions. Each of these should be given specific goals to fulfil their part of the total plan. In short the whole organisation is concentrated on what has to be done to succeed, with no overlap of responsibilities and with all unnecessary work discarded. Managers and workers can then be given incentives to exceed their budgeted targets for profits, and when these are exceeded they can earn increased bonuses. True dynamism is to do with managers having a supportive attitude to their subordinates. To illustrate this the way Lincoln Electric Co. used Time Study is instructive. In most companies Time Study people are used to check up on workers to make sure they are not loafing or making too much money for too little work. By contrast Lincoln said that the job of Time Study is to find a better way of doing a job and then to teach the workers to do it in the new way, for which they would be paid more money. In this way the Time Study people and the ordinary workers become a team helping each other. This civilised and entirely beneficial way of doing things should be inculcated throughout an organisation.

Industry is of the greatest importance to human beings because not only is it the basis of economic well-being but one's existence for much of life can be tied up in it. Hence a manager should make it the best they can. For this, vision is essential. Vision* is one of the highest human needs of Maslow and it is part of Nous and creativity: without it all human effort becomes third rate.

Vision, being one of the highest forms of creativity, has to have Creative Rapture in it; it has to have poetry. Rumi once wrote of a hen fostering a brood of ducklings, i.e. mystics, and therefore creatures of the mystic sea not the land. But I think of the visionary as being more than this; his mind soars like the fabulous homa bird or the heraldic bird of chivalry, the martlet. These birds never touch the earth, the martlet not even having feet. Vision is in all great minds. Newton's vision was celebrated in the work of the visionary architect E. L. Boullée, whose buildings have always inspired me with their magnificence. Compared to his Metropole, Versailles looks insignificant. At lower levels vision is part of all enterprise. At the end of this book I have tried to give a vision of retirement and the end of life as a contrast to the commonly accepted concept of dull, grey despair. I hope by this to show that vision is valid throughout life and universally.

James Lincoln's achievement is an example of the use of such vision. He had been the captain of a football team in an American university, and he never forgot the binding team spirit, the dedication to one another and the total lack of any need of supervision. He had the vision of achieving this in his own Electric Company that manufactured welding equipment. It resulted in the highest productivity rate I have ever heard about. This small company knocked the giant General Electric Company out of the welding business.

Managers have an entirely wrong idea of unions. A union reflects the attitude of employees to their company. In this sense a union is a figment. There is a graphic example of this fact. A large manufacturing company in America had the most terrible human relations. Trouble-makers of the worst sort were elected by employees as shop stewards. There was endless disruption and what Americans call wildcat strikes (unofficial stoppages) and disputes. One of the Directors said to his colleagues that clearly what they were doing was not working very well. He suggested a complete revolution in company thinking. They would treat the employees as reasonable and intelligent people. As friends, the employees would be kept informed. In disputes, if management was in the wrong, they would admit it and immediately redress the grievance. After two years the company was awarded a commendation for its outstanding human relations. At elections the trouble-makers were thrown out by the ordinary employees and very sensible and level-headed people were made shop stewards instead. There were no further wildcat strikes and disputes settled to a normal level. Nothing else was changed, only management's attitude and actions.

There is a very large body of writing on human relations starting with the work of Elton Mayo about 1900, who in essentials solved bad human relations. Only the Japanese have made much use of this information.

I should like to add the need for having the minimum of workers and the maximum of responsibility. This implies job enhancement or job enrichment.

Parkinson's Law has the cynical statement: "Work expands to fill the time allotted for its completion." Work is almost infinitely expandable or compressible. I used to tell employees that if we had the minimum people we could pay them more and give them greater security. Furthermore we could make their jobs more interesting and fulfilling. Whenever someone left, therefore, we automatically discussed how the job might be reallocated, with the object of increased payments and job satisfaction.

Job enrichment can take surprising forms. The canteen in our company was always a source of complaint. Running such an operation is never likely to inspire an ambitious manager. We transferred the entire operation to the employees on the work floor. They elected their own committee, who decided on what they would eat and made all the arrangements. It immediately improved and we as a company found that it was costing us less. The employees were delighted with the food, and their sense of achievement in doing better than the company knew no bounds.

A company increased the responsibility of its sales force; it gave them authorisation to replace faulty goods etc. Above all they were able to negotiate pricing. The sales improved markedly and this was not at any extra cost, the salesmen negotiating very sensibly. One manager was asked if he ever worried that he had given too much responsibility and the workers would violate that trust. He said that if he didn't lie awake at night, it would mean that he hadn't really given them much responsibility. In fact none of the managers reported any lack of responsibility, the salesmen all bringing a very mature attitude to their work.

This chapter had the aim of showing how the principles of Nous as Creative Intelligence may be applied to an entire organisation, making it more successful and far more dynamic. It is an example also of how new ideas meet grave obstacles of comprehension, because I had the utmost difficulty making my superiors understand the principles. In fact it was not until I was put in charge of a company that I was able to apply them fully. The results astonished the old managers. Productivity much more than doubled in two years and the previous losses were changed into spectacular profits. No words can do justice to the enthusiasm and new-found creativity of employees throughout the organisation.

I discuss the inability of minds to see new ideas in Chapter 8, "The Open and The Shut Mind".

Chapter 7
Creativity

Edward de Bono wrote a number of books outlining his system of lateral thinking. This is a basic method in which students are taught to solve small problems such as making four knives bridge the gap between three upright bottles. The blades of the knives are intertwined so that they form a platform on which a glass of water may be balanced. In fact the fourth knife is a red herring; it is unnecessary and is included just to complicate the solution. Another problem, after various modifications of the knife problem are solved, is one involving oblong blocks, which are made to touch in certain ways. More and more difficult examples are included. Finally he has what he called his L Game: a small game like noughts and crosses but more challenging.

In another of his books he includes the old problem of the young daughter of a debtor who is coveted by the money lender. He offers to waive the debt if she chooses the white pebble in a box, but if she chooses the black pebble she has to marry him. The sharp-eyed girl notices with horror that the money lender puts two black pebbles in the box, which he had taken from the path of black and white pebbles. What does she do to escape the clutches of the money lender and save her father from his debt? This requires a different way of thinking – lateral thinking.

For someone starting on learning creativity, de Bono's *Five Day Course in Thinking* is a good introduction. It does not go much into intuition and there is nothing on Nous, Higher Intelligence or indeed Non-Aristotelian Thinking. It is, however, a good preliminary to the work of W. J. J. Gordon's *Synectics* discussed in this chapter. It was claimed for lateral thinking that it increased the I.Q. of Venezuelan children, where it was adopted. Furthermore it undoubtedly helps to get students out of their ruts of conventional thinking, which can only do good.

In his book *Act of Creation* Arthur Koestler wrote that creativity comes from a breach between thought compartments; a creative idea does not come from orderly thought but a breach by which an idea that is normally part of one compartment of the brain is applied to another, entailing surprise. A joke, which is a low form of creativity, makes use of this fact and we laugh at its incongruity. But creativity is much more than a mere juggling of ideas and words; I mention this because some people think it comes from random thought.

W. J. J. Gordon wrote a book called *Synectics* that is a detailed way of producing ideas. Ideas do not come from making the strange familiar, which is the usual way to understand something that puzzles the mind; rather they come from the opposite mental process of making the familiar strange by distorting and reversing the usual way we look at the world, this being achieved by making analogies.

For instance, when physicists speak of light travelling in waves the analogy comes from the sea. Marc Isambard Brunel watched a ship worm tunnelling through wood, and he got the idea of caissons from it, for the worm made a tube for itself as it went forward. Caissons for underwater construction came from direct analogy.

Other forms of analogy are used; for example, the inventor of the altimeter used personal analogy by imagining himself to be a spring and going through the same contortions as the spring so that he could gain an insight into how it might work and solve his problem. Analogies come mostly from nature but they can come from any source, such as fabulous animals and magic carpets. All these analogies can be applied to inventions as well as poetry, which follows the same principles as invention using similes and metaphors.

Gordon gave an account of an invention in which the inventor wrote down his thoughts and psychological states as the solution came to him. This account is important not just for its insight into creativity, but also because if people themselves can use the principles of inventing, they are half-way to understanding Non-Aristotelian Thinking and also Realization.

The problem the altimeter inventor was faced with was given to him by his government. Many accidents occur in the air through pilots misreading altimeters that have double dial faces, as in figure 1, but the human eye is rarely confused if one of the indicators is a dial and the other a band, as in figure 2. Furthermore the old solution to the problem entailed using innumerable gears and little wheels that were a source of inaccuracy, especially when they began to wear out. What he had to do was devise a dial that would abolish both the psychological reading error and the wear error of the gears, as in figure 3.

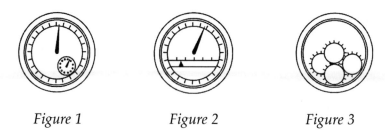

| *Figure 1* | *Figure 2* | *Figure 3* |

First the inventor considered what was not needed in the mass of gears and machinery. The one thing that was essential was the master spring, the rest he discarded. When he thought about springs he felt himself to be far away from the problem. He considered what it must feel like to be a spring; he imagined himself folding in and out like a spring. He thought about this for some time and then decided that he had done enough thinking and needed to get away from the problem and look at it from a distance. Much later he began to think only about the spring and how it would have to move so that a band would be shown on the dial. He considered the movement of an enormous spring. When he held it at one end and wound it, the spring would go in and out. He then asked himself what would happen if he put a blob of ink on the spring. As the spring expanded and contracted, the blob would move in as the spring contracted and out when it expanded.

He then thought of the spring as being on its own and completely outside him; it was no longer anything to do with him. If he put a spot on the spring it described a shallow arc, which was what he was looking for:

While solving the problem, he had experienced the following five psychological states:

1.   Detachment, in which he felt cut off, as though he viewed the problem from far away.

2.   Involvement, so that he became the spring and felt his body twisting as if he were the spring.

3.   Deferment, so that he avoided a premature solution, which would probably be a poor one.

4.   Meditation, reverie and free thinking, in which his mind was allowed to run free.

5.   An indescribable feeling in which the solution appeared to be on its own.

In his book *Genius*, Eysenck writes of many creative people going through similar experiences. Poincaré, the great French mathematician, was one of these who described his process of thinking very clearly. The method is universal: first there is the preliminary labour; next the incubation period; then the sudden integration, owing its existence to inspiration or intuition not logical thought; and finally verification or proof, which is conscious.

Gordon laid much stress on the use of Synectics Groups of five or six people who are given a specific problem to solve. These groups work in 'brain-storming' sessions in which recorders are used. The members are encouraged to utter outrageous statements in the hope that they will trigger off new ideas; the thought behind this is that ideas come from random thought. This is in fact mistaken, as is confirmed in Eysenck's book on genius. It will be recalled that reverie and free thinking were part of the method of the altimeter inventor, as well as visualisation, which together with intuition are the vital requirements for invention. Answers rarely come in the busy hours of work; rather they are the products of long walks, meditations and daydreams; etc. If by some lucky chance an idea comes out of random thought, it will not be a very deep one.

The really great ideas do not come easily or quickly. A problem has to be thought about for a long time and the mind must be allowed to speculate and enter reveries. At length, and often when least expected, the answer comes. Charles Darwin had the first inkling of his theory of the origin of species in South America; later in the Galapagos Islands it took firmer root, but it was only many years later that he was able to formulate the entire theory. Similarly Albert Einstein took many years over his general Theory of Relativity.

Gordon's system of analogies, though an advance over Koestler's method, is only a lesser form of creativity. André Gide startled me when I read in his *Journal* that he had used no metaphors in his book *The Fruits of the Earth* (*Les Nourritures Terrestres*), his most creative book. Now metaphor is the poetic form of analogy, and since I had supposed that metaphor was the height of poetic expression, my surprise could not have been greater. I thought about this for a long time and decided that Gide was referring to puerile analogy.

The creative person must enter the Unspeakable and must translate what they feel into words. Some feelings may be translated without visual images but most of it has to be visual and this requires metaphor; moreover mystic poetry, which is about regions where words run out, requires metaphor, for nothing else can give any idea of what the mystic feels. Gide clearly referred to metaphors made by someone who had not fulfilled the requirements of creative thought so they were no more than clever verbal imagery.

Feelings of the utmost pleasure and joy come from creativity. Gide wrote in his *Journal* that he never regained the rapture he felt during the writing of *The Fruits of the Earth*. Gordon wrote about Hedonic Response as being one of the authentic joys of creativity and the Peak Experience as another even higher joy. I have used the expression Creative Rapture for this experience. Creativity is usually achieved by entering the Unspeakable and this is accompanied by Hedonic Response springing from the mind's appreciation of beauty. When this feeling of excitement and joy arises, the poet or creative person know that they are on the right track; in fact it acts like the scent to a hound. Later when the solution or creative idea comes they may feel the full joy of the Peak Experience.

These feelings are not confined to poets and artists; rather they are universal and they are to be found in all creative people. For instance, scientists insist that this feeling of beauty is part of all great discoveries. Physicist James Clerk Maxwell's proofs were extolled for their beauty; Einstein's theories were said to have a grandeur and beauty that gave them authenticity long before tests could be made to prove them. Bertrand Russell wrote that higher mathematics has an austere beauty like architecture.

In contrast to the prosaic account of the altimeter inventor described earlier, here is Friedrich August Kekulé's description of how he discovered the Structural Theory:

> One beautiful summer evening I was riding on the last omnibus through the deserted streets usually so filled with life. I rode as usual on the outside of the omnibus. I fell into a reverie. Atoms flitted before my eyes. I had never before succeeded in perceiving their manner of moving. That evening, however, I saw that frequently two smaller atoms were coupled together, that larger ones seized the two smaller ones, that still larger ones held fast three and even four of the smaller ones and that all were whirled around in a bewildering dance. I saw how the larger atoms formed a row and one dragged along still smaller ones at the ends of the chain … The cry "Clapham Road" waked me from my reverie, but I spent a part of the night writing down sketches of these dream pictures.
>
> (quoted in Gordon, *Synectics*)

Thus arose the Structural Theory.

The sheer joys of creativity are said to be pursued by some scientists as if they were almost the only aim in life. I read of a mathematician whose work is encoding to prevent fraud in credit card transactions. He said that prior to taking up this work, he had been at a university and if anyone had suggested that what he was doing could be useful, he would have been mortified: he regarded himself as an artist. In the same way the mathematician Sir Godfrey Hardy hoped that nothing he did would be useful.

Gordon and Maslow used the expression Hedonic Response. I prefer the less academic and to me more accurate term Creative Rapture. Gordon had two definitions for this phenomenon:

> 1. It is a pleasurable feeling developed towards the successful conclusion of a period of problem solving concentration, that signals the conceptual presence of a major new viewpoint, which promises to lead to a solution. 2. It is a pleasurable feeling which occurs in a minor way acting as a moment-to-moment evaluation of the creative process itself.

The sense of joy in creativity is a harbinger of solutions to problems. It is an emotion that should be cultivated. Most, if not all, creative people have been aware of it and used it. Many of them made comments about it. Gordon and Maslow wrote much about it, others including Poincaré, Blake, Edison, Sir Joshua Reynolds, Einstein, Thoreau, are just a few of many who referred to it.

Einstein used it as a guide: as soon as he apprehended a problem, he seemed to feel instinctively the direction in which the solution might lie. For others the feeling brought on the thought that they were on the right track. When Faraday was led by this feeling in a direction contrary to the laws of electricity of his time, he would ignore the laws and follow his own instincts. He said that "the laws of his day did very great injury to science by contracting and limiting the habitual views of those engaged in pursuing it" (J. A. Crowther, *Michael Faraday*).

Maslow wrote of this experience and its wonder in *Motivation and Personality*:

> Feelings of limitless horizons opening up to the vision, the feeling of being simultaneously more powerful and also more helpless than one had ever been before, the feeling of great ecstasy and wonder and awe, the loss of placing in time and space with, finally, the conviction that something

> extremely important had happened, so that the subject is to some extent transformed and strengthened even in his daily life by such experiences.

This experience can have varying degrees, it is not always the same: there can be intense ones and mild ones. It has been described as the highest order of excitement and some people are said to become addicted to it because of the joy of creativity and this excitement.

About creativity in general William Blake said: "You have the same intuition as I, only you do not trust or cultivate it. You can 'see' what I do, if you choose" (Alexander Gilchrist, *Life of William Blake*, 1880; quoted in Gordon, *Synectics*).

To illustrate how this feeling led to a solution, the account of an inventor with the problem of getting military tanks over chasms with ten-feet gaps between sides is of interest. The creative feeling had come to him and he had worked on the problem for a long time. He decided to get away from it all and drove a car into the countryside. Under a tree he was idly watching some ants working at the base of the tree. Suddenly he noticed how they were able to bridge a mini-chasm by one ant stretching across and another climbing over its back and thus reaching the far side. From this came his solution of connecting tanks together so that the lead one would reach across the chasm supported by the one behind. Then when it reached the far side it would pull the one behind across. In this way as many as six tanks all connected together could cross a chasm without the need of a bridge.

Gordon said that in his experience of teaching creativity in Synectics, solutions always came from aesthetics and never from logic. You can go further than this and say that all creativity comes from Creative Rapture. This is especially true of poetry, which is no more than a blueprint of a poet's ecstasy. A real poem is one that is forged in the fires of rapture, and if it is not, then it is probably no more than a sequence of words. It has been observed that scientific proofs and theories have a certain elegance, and it is not difficult to see why: they came out of the sense of the beautiful, hence they are bound to have elegance. As I mentioned before, creativity is the Elixir of Life; it is the driving force of all artistic people.

David Bohm, the double Nobel Prize winning physicist, said that creativity was a fundamental principle of the Cosmos and what needed to be explained were the processes that were not creative. Creativity is a primeval power from the origins of the Cosmos. When a person is creating they are nearest to their God; from being a mere slab of animated matter they are lifted among the demigods of creation. All those who create are aware that inspiration comes from outside them and that they are only a channel for creativity. Some people think it comes from the morphogenetic field, the Collective Unconscious or the Divine, etc. Indeed, creativity is a divine gift that expands human horizons and gives our thoughts wings; the poet breathes life into an idea and makes it immortal.

The creativity of scientists has one fundamental difference from other forms of creativity: it has been said that where one genius makes a great discovery four lesser people would eventually make the same discovery. Ideas accumulated at the time of Einstein's work on relativity. Whereas other scientists were caught up in their semantic and scientific trammels, the genius Einstein saw the problem clearly and was able to propound his theory. A scientist has to absorb much data and then after long thought they may make the breakthrough, so they have to overcome their prejudices and mental blocks as well as use creativity. It was in this way that the structure of DNA was mapped by Crick and Watson as recounted in the book *The Double Helix* of James D. Watson.

Creativity uses visualisation, very careful perception and free thinking in the form of reveries and daydreams; indeed exactly the same way of thinking is used to master Realization – the seeing of reality. This gives much hope because Gordon found that using Synectics, creativity could be taught; in fact his students won important prizes in literature as well as made inventions.

Creativity is not rare in the population; rather it is widespread and common. It is therefore one of the best ways to master Non-Aristotelian Thinking and Realization. All an aspirant has to do is use introspection and analyse their thoughts after achieving a breakthrough and it is possible that Realization will come to them.

Once the principles of creativity have been understood, the best way to proceed further is by studying accounts of actual inventions.

I shall give examples from different fields such as science, business and poetry.

Many ideas come in reveries and daydreams such as the often mentioned reverie of Friedrich August Kekulé when he discovered the Structural Theory, described earlier. A similar discovery was achieved in another reverie, which led to his finding the structure of the Benzene Ring. He saw atoms flitting before his eyes; they were in long lines like serpents. "And see! What was that? One of the serpents seized its own tail and the form whirled mockingly before my eyes. I was awake in a flash." He spent that night making sketches of the dream pictures and working out the implications of the hypothesis.

Thomas Alva Edison invented the gramophone in 1877. Many years before he had experimented with sending a telegraph message from a rotating disc. When it whirled at high speed a hum was heard. In 1877 he made a funnel-shaped toy. When he talked into the funnel, vibrations caused by his voice worked a mechanism, which had a man sawing a log. At times the man moved rhythmically and at other times jerkily depending on the words shouted at the funnel and the pitch of his voice. From the musical hum remembered from years previously and the man sawing his log came the flash of insight that enabled Edison to produce a gramophone in 30 hours.

Accident and good luck play a large part in some inventions; here what is needed is keen perception and insight. For instance the drug penicillin was discovered by Alexander Fleming who noticed a green mould destroying germs on a specimen plate. To most people it would have been an irrelevance – an unknown mould invading what had been a different experiment.

In a similar way, Charles Goodyear by accident burnt some rubber mixed with sulphur. He was the only person present who was able to see the significance of the strange substance he had made. It resulted in the process called vulcanising, which enabled rubber to withstand high temperatures.

Other inventions owed little or nothing to luck. Alexander Graham Bell noticed that the bones of the human ear are massive compared to the thin membrane that operates them. The thought came to him that if this was so, a thicker membrane could also operate a piece of steel; this led to the invention of the telephone. A very beneficial discovery that has saved countless lives as well as preventing untold misery was that of Edward Jenner, a country doctor of medicine. He investigated the popular belief that milk-maids never got smallpox. Despite much opposition and after overcoming difficulties with faulty serum, he proved his idea of vaccination by trying it on a boy using matter from a cowpox sore.

With the expansion of education in science, engineering and other fields inventions are burgeoning. Radio, TV, computers, micro-processors, jet engines, rockets and antibiotics are only a few of them. In industry new processes abound, such as Pilkington's float glass made by pouring molten glass over a bed of liquid lead and Rolls-Royce's growing crystals of steel for stronger turbine blades.

In art and poetry the creative person must escape from the commonplace view of the world. The artist Turner had himself lashed to the mast of a ship in a storm so that he could see what it was really like. Keats did something similar by throwing himself into the sea so that he could write about it better.

Poetic creativity follows the same rules as scientific creativity using metaphor and simile in place of analogy. For instance, Shakespeare used metaphor when he wrote of England as "this precious stone set in the silver sea". Similarly Dylan Thomas wrote in his poem "Fern Hill": "Time held me green and dying / Though I sang in my chains like the sea".

Henry David Thoreau is a good writer for students of creativity to study because he had a metaphorical way of writing. About the American bird the bobolink he wrote in his *Journal*: "It is as if he touched his harp within a vase of liquid melody and when he took it out, the notes fell from the trembling strings . . . It is the foretaste of such strains as never fell on mortal ears, to hear which we should rush to our doors and contribute all that we possess and are."

Creativity is used not only for solving problems in business but also in strategy, which is the prime role of a Chief Executive. When they are doing routine work, they are neglecting their main function, which is to think. Just as great pleasure comes from the solving of problems, it is to be found in abundance in strategic thinking, which must be creative or it is worthless.

The whole subject of business strategy has given me the highest pleasure I gained in business. There is much to learn about matters such as product life cycles, trade cycles, and methods of diversification. The organisation of a company is itself a matter of strategy because it must be designed for survival over the long term. It has to have three distinct and separate organisations – the operational, the entrepreneurial and the strategic, and these cannot be organised in the same way. For instance the strategic organisation must be a small group led by the Chief Executive, who do practically nothing except work out the future of the company. In this short book, I do not intend to go into this except to point out that it requires much study, but it is the most stimulating and intellectually rewarding part of business; it can lift work into an art.

The strategic aims of different companies must be totally different because their problems are different. The strategic executive of a company, using creative thought, must discover what the vital needs of the company are to succeed in its industry over the long term. RTZ in its mining operations in far-off countries had the strategy of giving nationals of the country in which they operated the maximum ownership without RTZ losing control; they kept just over 50% of the stock. They feared the nationalism of governments so it was vital for them to have as much local support as they could.

Glaxo had to have a steady stream of new drugs in the pipeline to take over when patents ran out on their breadwinners. All their creative ability and energy had to be put into research and development; for them to bring other parts of the company, such as production or administration, up to expert level would be a waste of energy and brains. These other parts of the company could never make a decisive impact on the future wellbeing of the company so they needed to be only competent.

A famous Chief Executive described himself as a captain on the bridge of an ocean liner looking out for reefs and icebergs, while the rest of the employees were down in the engine room.

Threats to companies can come from many sources, including the unexpected, such as stock raiders. The most dangerous threat is often from an entirely different technology: ice distributors were destroyed by refrigerators and freezers; portrait painters by cameras.

Theodore Levitt, in his book *Innovations in Management*, illustrated this danger by an account of the oil industry, which always lacked strategy. They were so busy telling everyone what a great industry they were that they repeatedly ran out of business. The original product was paraffin for lamps, which they gave away to the population of a backward country, counting on the demand for paraffin to fill them. They were going along merrily never thinking about the future when they were surprised by the gas light, followed by the electric light. Providentially they were rescued on one occasion by the paraffin stove invented by someone far from the oil industry's narrow purview. On another occasion they were saved by an inventor in a distant country in an entirely different industry: the internal combustion engine gave the oil industry its greatest growth but with absolutely no credit to the oil industry.

War, for its insights both into creativity and strategy, is a fertile field of study for anyone interested in creativity. Innumerable have been the inventions in war, starting with bows and arrows and continuing to this day with lasers, smart bombs, night sights and so on. In fact war gives a tremendous impetus to invention.

The study of the battles and campaigns of great generals such as Tamerlane, Hannibal and Alexander the Great can provide rich insight into strategy and tactics. Let me give an example of a strategy that Wellington used in his battles with Napoleon's generals in Portugal and Spain. He gave orders that the local population must not be harmed in any way. He had learnt from his earlier campaigns in India that a foreign army must have the local population on its side, or at least neutral. All produce was paid for, all damage and injury redressed and the population was safe. In contrast the French ransacked the countryside stealing everything they could lay their hands on. In consequence the local people were not antagonistic to the British; indeed at the Battle of Busaco, the French were short of food for this very reason.

Karl Popper described science as the greatest adventure because it is an endless search for new ideas. There is no reason why business and other human activities cannot be adventures; it requires only the harnessing of the Higher Intelligence and creativity. In fact creativity is a vital need of human beings at the highest levels of self-fulfilment. Maslow made an interesting investigation into this. He wanted to find out what constituted mental health. He knew that he could not discover this by reading studies into human psychology because all this work had been done on sick and neurotic people. So he had to make his own inquiries using his own subjects; these he found among friends and associates whom he knew to be well adjusted and self-assured; they had no chips on their shoulders.

He found that they saw reality more accurately than neurotic people because their judgements were not swayed by fears and hopes, which unbalance the thinking of neurotics. Furthermore they had more curiosity and vitality; and they had regained the joy of childhood. Many of them were artistic and poetic thus fulfilling the highest needs of the beautiful and the Peak Experience, which come only from creativity. They had passed beyond the mere gaining of power and money; so much so that they did not worry any more over their shortcomings, which were now thought of simply as idiosyncrasies of no real importance. They were civilised people in the best sense of the word. It is no exaggeration to think of creativity as being one of the greatest civilising influences of the world.

Popper also made a suggestion about scientific method that was completely at odds with the classic method deriving from Bacon and Mill. It liberates scientists from the fear that their theory will be destroyed, taking with it all that they have worked on for years. It removes the desperate clinging of scientists to their own theory or hypothesis, which also makes it difficult for them to see anyone else's idea.

The true scientific method is revolutionary in that progress is made through replacing a hypothesis with a new one more in accord with facts. The old method was by observation and it entailed saving a hypothesis. In contrast the new method is about actively trying to falsify a theory – it is the critical method. Once a scientist has grasped that this is how things stand, they will adopt a critical attitude to their own pet theory. They will prefer to test it themselves and even falsify it, rather than leave this to their critics. Popper wrote about his friend the brain scientist Sir John Eccles, who recorded his gratitude to Popper in his Nobel Prize biography. Eccles had worked on the method of transmission of stimuli across synapses, his position being that it was done mainly electrically. His rivals at Cambridge, Sir Henry Dale and his team, argued that it was done chemically. In time Eccles saw that he was going to be defeated and this very much depressed him. He then learnt of Popper's method, that stated how it was not disgraceful to have one's hypothesis falsified. He called this the best news he had heard for years. He had at last experienced the great liberating power of Popper's teachings on scientific method. Later in this same biography he wrote: "Now I can even rejoice in the falsification of a hypothesis I have cherished as my brain-child, for such falsification is a scientific success" (from Popper's *All Life Is Problem Solving*).

Later it was found that he had abandoned his hypothesis prematurely: there were synapses that used electrical and others that used chemical transmission.

Chapter 8
The Open and The Shut Mind

Throughout the history of science, creative minds have made great discoveries but have had difficulty getting them accepted. This is analogous to trying to explain Non-Aristotelian Thinking or Realization taught by the Buddha and Plato* 2,500 years ago, which met the same blindness by most people.

In the book *Genius* by Hans Eysenck there are some insights into this problem. J. Z. Young's observation will be recalled of a man blind from birth who learns to see as an adult for the first time, finding difficulty recognising anything in the confusion of light and other sense data. It takes him some time before he can see properly. This he does by activating a screen or filter to exclude irrelevant information so that he can concentrate on what is important for him. This enables him to recognise things but it hampers accurate seeing. In fact this filtering or screening is a cause of our blindness to new ideas.

A schizophrenic has a faulty filter, which allows too much data, internal and external, to reach their mind so it is overwhelmed. Their filter does not exclude voices and other irrelevant thoughts; they have a wide field of view, indeed it is too wide.

Creative people have this same wide field of view but they are able to distinguish relevant from irrelevant information. Some of the most creative people, such as geniuses, are described as having psychopathic tendencies.

Ordinary uncreative people with high or low I.Q.'s have too effective a screen or filter making them impermeable to new ideas; unfortunately this is a large proportion of the human race. They have tunnel vision. The damage such people cause is immense, especially when they get into positions of power and influence; furthermore, the higher their intelligence the more damage they can do.

Plato is viewed in the East in a much more mystical light than in the west. His teaching came via the neo-platonists who were thrown out of Athens by Justinian and took refuge in the Court of Nurshirvan the Just of Persia, where they imparted their knowledge.

In science there are innumerable stories of creative people suffering from this blindness of superiors and officials.

Ignaz Semmelweis was a doctor in a maternity hospital in Vienna in the 1840s. He noticed that trainee doctors were not washing their hands between examinations and thus spreading puerperal fever among patients, causing 25% mortality. He instituted hygiene measures, namely soap and water and later antiseptics. (He was the originator of antiseptics.) Mortality immediately dropped to a normal level of a few percentage points. The head of the maternity hospital, Klein, through blind jealousy, stopped the hygiene measures resulting in a return to the high mortality levels before the experiments were instituted. Furthermore he stopped Semmelweis's promotion and finally hounded him out of Vienna.

Most people have heard of the opposition Galileo met from the Church. Even worse was that of Giordano Bruno who, for the same heliocentric views as Galileo, was burnt at the stake in 1600. Max Planck, the discoverer of quantum theory, could not get any of his professors or anyone else to understand his work. He said that it was necessary for his generation to die out before another generation might understand such ideas. These are only a few of countless examples of the same blindness, and this is not just in science; for instance the engineer Frank Whittle had his jet aero engine turned down by the official mind.

Even worse is for creative ideas to be sent to a committee to appraise, as is now the case with funding for university ideas. A committee by its very nature is guaranteed not to be able to see a new idea, especially if it is a revolutionary one.

Some factors have been found to influence the extent of creativity. I.Q. is not decisive but it is needed up to about 120, beyond which it does not correlate well with creativity; in fact there are large numbers of people with very high I.Q. who are totally uncreative. The wide field of view that was mentioned earlier is vital. Persistence and hard work are essential – Edison spoke of the need for 90% perspiration and 10% inspiration. Inventors must have self-assurance and determination and not be discouraged by adverse criticism. They need to be rebels and nonconformists; the celebrated English eccentric is the type of the creative person.

The Blind Men and the Elephant

Each one is led to a different part of the elephant to feel it. One thinks the ear is a winnowing basket; another that the leg is a pillar; another that the trunk is a hose and so on. The deeper meaning of this ancient story is that human beings are no better than the blind men. We may have eyes but we do not see correctly. It is as if we see through distorting lenses, the distortions being caused by a haze of memory and words.

Races with the best and worst results in winning Nobel Prizes are instructive. Jews, in proportion to their total population, have won an amazing number of these prizes. Considering the various criteria needed in creativity, it can be seen that Jews except in their relatively new homeland of Israel have been outsiders everywhere for thousands of years. They have had to possess self-reliance and individualism. They also have a tradition of deep learning helped no doubt by their exclusion from ordinary occupations, which forced them into cerebral work such as finance and the professions: brain work was always essential for them. Furthermore, persecution through the ages has induced them to keep their thoughts to themselves, hence they have tended towards introversion.

By comparison Japanese, who supposedly possess higher I.Q.'s than Caucasian peoples, have produced few Nobel Prize winners. Here it can be seen that the Japanese are utterly different from Jews in that they are highly homogeneous and tend to conform. In business a worker is viewed with the utmost suspicion and resentment if they seek to leave their company to join another. Team effort rather than individual effort is almost a religion in Japan.

Failure to create or see new ideas stems from two sources: the filter or screen mentioned earlier and Aristotelian Thinking. These may in fact be just one mechanism – the Aristotelian. Aristotelian Thinking is the way the mind excludes the unfamiliar; it is about recognising things or finding resemblances, called Associative Thinking by Abraham Maslow. It is roughly analogous to the search that is made in a filing cabinet. The phrase "racking one's brains" describes this often hopeless search. Unfortunately a truly revolutionary new idea cannot be in the filing cabinet at all. Thus Aristotelian Thinking is incapable of grasping a new idea that is revolutionary.

Gordon wrote that in his Synectics groups, no creative ideas came if over 50% of members were technical experts. Technical knowledge coupled with Aristotelian Thinking prevents ideas, whereas laymen in these groups, having no burden of expert knowledge, had none of the inhibitions of the experts.

But using Non-Aristotelian Thinking, the mind is made to ferret out, in Maslow's phrase, the intrinsic nature of an idea, which gives the mind the possibility of mastering it. Here the use of the Structural Differential of Korzybski is invaluable. It forces the mind to look intently, then pause and visualise and use intuition. In this way the mind may be able to overcome its obsession with the familiar so that the new idea may be seen.

There seems to be another factor in Aristotelian Thinking that contributes to the failure to see new ideas and to create. There is evidence that the overriding of sense impressions by the mind and memory leads to disuse of the perceptive faculty. Years ago when I was a tea taster I was amazed to learn that 80% of American men and 70% of American women could not distinguish the four primary tastes (sweet, sour, salty and bitter) in a blind test. These people over a long period had clearly never tasted their food, simply gobbling it down so their taste buds fell into disuse. A similar condition may be at work in the higher senses, the mind and memory not merely overruling the senses but submerging them.

Maslow's way of seeing revolutionary new ideas can be applied to seeing Non-Aristotelian Thinking, which itself is a revolutionary idea – though by no means new, for Plato and the Buddha were aware of it. It requires Maslow's ferreting out its intrinsic meaning; it can never be found in the mind's memory file.

Maslow's way of looking at things can be applied to any of the blindnesses of people, such as failure to appreciate art or poetry. However, it is useless, it seems, to help those who are afflicted with the Shut Mind and cannot see their own lack of perception. They are unfortunates who live blinkered lives, imprisoned within the narrow boundaries of their minds, victims of the verbal illusion.

It is interesting to consider the time when children change from thinking about the real world and become verbalisers. I recall my own childhood when I felt a definite division between the verbal world of adults and schooling, and what I considered the actual world of games, bird nesting, fishing, shooting and excursions. I still remember vividly in my teens being surprised to discover that words purported to refer to the real world more or less accurately. But even then and thereafter I always felt suspicion towards facile speakers, those who were never at a loss for words. They had no burden of having to translate visual images and sensing into words; in other words they were pure verbalisers, whose whole world was of words.

I knew that they were very prone to make the most ridiculous decisions in practical matters. Later in the army I came upon academic officers who were word perfect in theory but lacked strategy and imagination.

Aristotelian thinkers such as politicians were called various phrases such as "Superior Imbeciles" by Korzybski. He blamed them for most of our human problems. Krishnamurti, as we saw earlier, was also critical, saying that their minds were muddled with problems so they caused even greater problems. Another Realized person, Thoreau, was one of the most creative people in America. He reported that his fellow villagers of Concord, New Hampshire considered him the "humblest, cheapest, least dignified man in the village". They pitied him for his "mean and unfortunate destiny". But as he wrote, he could not hesitate in his choice. For him his way of life was the only Elysium. For his part he asked in what respect a village was superior to a village of prairie dogs.*

We should not be discouraged if we find ourselves alone in our thinking. Sir Karl Popper had a most effective answer to this common experience of original thinkers. It was in his book The World of Parmenides that he wrote about the need for swimming against the tide of popular thought. He added that even if our ideas become accepted, we should continue to swim against the tide: "The attempt to swim against the tide may sometimes lead to unexpected situations. For example, a philosopher or scientist may be struck by the calamity that his own ideas become fashionable. An experienced swimmer against the tide will, however, know what to do should he ever find himself in this envied but unenviable position. He will simply continue his favourite exercise, even if it means swimming against the tide of his own followers."

Chapter 9
Seeing the Real and the Beautiful:
Rationale for the Unspeakable and the Transcendent

In this book I have shown various methods by which a person might escape from the verbal and memory prison in which most of the world, unknown to themselves, is trapped. Mastery of both creativity and Non-Aristotelian Thinking is prevented by a failure to believe that thought is possible in such non-verbal worlds as the Unspeakable and the Transcendent. Some of the most advanced scientists such as David Bohm write of these regions beyond the senses. For instance, Sir Roger Penrose in an interview in India said that there were three worlds:

> The [first world] is the world of our conscious perceptions, yet it is the world that we know least about in any kind of precise scientific terms. It is a world containing mental images of chairs and tables ... and where smells and sounds and sensations of all kinds intermingle with our thoughts and decisions to act. There are two other worlds that we are cognizant of – less directly than the former – but which we know quite a lot about. One is the physical world, which contains actual chairs and tables, TV sets, cars, butterflies and actions of neurons. It is not at all clear why the world of our perceptions should have anything to do with the physical world, but apparently it does.
>
> There is one other kind of world, though many find difficulty in accepting its actual existence: the Platonic world of mathematical forms. There we find the natural numbers 0, 1, 2, 3, and so on and the algebra of complex numbers. ... The existence of this last world rests on the profound, timeless, and universal nature of these concepts, and the fact that their laws are independent of those who discover them.
>
> (from a newspaper report, India, 1998)

In his book *A New Science of Life*, Dr Rupert Sheldrake argued that natural forms do not come entirely from DNA but also from an influence outside called the morphogenetic field. Previous examples of a form influence the new form by morphic resonance, in a similar way to a TV set picking up signals on the airwaves from a distant transmitter. A previous unrelated experiment tends to verify this theory. It was done in New York where rats were trained to perform certain actions. Not only did rats, which were trained to do these actions some time after the first tests, learn to do them much faster, but it was found that later on in Edinburgh rats were doing progressively better on the same experiments; later still in Australia rats were learning still faster. Somehow rats world-wide were learning from each other.

Another argument endorsing learning at a distance came from experience with the formation of crystals. When a new solution is made to crystallise, it takes some time before it can do this successfully. On occasion it is necessary to put a particle of a crystal into the solution to "instruct" it. As time goes on it becomes easier; again this improvement is world-wide. As someone pointed out, it was as if particles of crystals on the beards of itinerant scientists were causing crystallisation world-wide.

Telepathy is another example of communication at a distance. Not only did primitive savages often have this ability but some modern people also. The fact of scientific discovery being achieved at the same time by different scientists far away from each other and not in communication adds to this argument.

Some of the history of science has been about discoveries that were considered miraculous – that is, discovering things beyond the senses such as X-rays, radio waves, cosmic waves, etc.

Worlds beyond the senses have been a firm belief of mystics since the beginnings of history; in a way it is the same as the worlds of imagination of poetry. Ibnal-Arabi, who was called the Son of Plato, took the idea of the archetypes from Plato. Another person influenced by the same idea was Carl Jung, leading to the Collective Unconscious, which is not unlike the morphogenetic field of biologists. Some people will never accept such ideas because it requires imagination and use of the Higher Intelligence, including intuition.

These worlds are a sanctuary from the narrow world of materialism. Robert Lynd wrote what I have always thought of as the best introduction to the world of poetic imagination, which has influenced me all my life. He made some of his points using nursery rhymes. Whereas Little Jack Horner is prose – it does not make the world a new place for us – Ride-A-Cock-Horse and The Little Nut Tree are poetry. They take us into a world that is outside the four walls of our material existence. The first of these tells of a woman with rings on her fingers and bells on her toes, and she would have music wherever she goes. And the Little Nut Tree could only bear a silver nutmeg and a golden pear, but "The King of Spain's daughter/Came to visit me,/And all for the sake/Of my little nut tree." The poet grows wings like a bird, imagination's wings, and becomes free in an infinite world. Mystic poetry takes us still further into a pure world of the imagination where nothing verbal or material exists: it is the ultimate unassailable wilderness.

This is the homeland of the mystic, which occurs often in the night. To wake up in the midnight hours can be pure joy. They can be a Golconda of spiritual riches. This is what Rumi wrote about pain, whose virtue is to wake the mystic so that they won't slumber all night like a buffalo and miss the rapture of the nights. For a time I used the nights in this way to achieve creative ideas. I gained the rapture that Rumi wrote about, but I found that I had lost the habit of sleep. Perhaps such a practice was easier in Rumi's day than in our modern world. Better I think is to use the nights as a non-verbal region of Nous: a poetic and mystic world of the Emerald Cities and the Orient, a time of spiritual recreation not work.

Non-Aristotelian Thinking is not just another way of thinking, it leads to a totally different way of living. This is what Realization means. A person who *sees* will never be the same again because life becomes transformed. Furthermore the aspirant at first will see only a small portion of what they will eventually see. As they progress so they will part further and further from the way they used to live. In fact there is no end to this change – to become a being of the Orient is only one of the experiences of this state, which is utterly limitless. New vistas and new countries appear and in turn give way to more and more wonderful experiences.

Rumi wrote of rapture in a story of a man who beat his drum at midnight causing complaints from his neighbours. In reply he said:

> To you it's night, to me that same night is morningtide.
> To you it's prison, to me that prison is like a garden–
> Your feet are in the mud, to me the mud has become roses.
> You have mourning: I have feasting and drums.

The darkness of the night is a blackboard on which, as children once more, we write hieroglyphs of light. We can play for ever in the fields of the Lord. This is the utmost release. The materialist, however successful in riches and material objects, is a prisoner in the narrow confines of their material world. Pleasures may distract them and possessions give transitory satisfaction but in the end it will all turn to ashes. For a mystic there is no such disappointment; their riches are incorruptible, and indeed in old is when their gardens especially blossom.

One of the oldest scriptures of the world says: "Lead me from the Unreal to the Real" (*Brh Upanishad*).

Once the real is known life becomes joy and bliss. When we learn to look beyond the veils of memory and words, the world is transformed. Every day with the poet we can be at the gates of paradise.

Days of snow and ice can be instructive. I sense the wonder and silence of snow. In the night a wonderland is created. The sun's heat soon loosens the clasps and bangles of the ice jewellery and they start to fall about me – jewels of the freezing night. What we should see is that the everyday world is far more wonderful; it is only unfamiliarity that makes us think of the snow scene as being especially astonishing.

To see the real we must perceive acutely and use our Nous, which is a therapeutic way of thinking. A novice should embark on it by going to unfamiliar places such as an unknown garden or landscape. It must be seen as an utterly strange place, where nothing is what we think it is. What is before us is not the naive world of ordinary people where hard objects seem to stand out from a solid earth, but particles of light, arrows of light, streaming into our eyes, which like subtle prisms split and rearrange the light into pictures. The tapestry before us is of woven light. Everything is held in that light like butterflies pinned in a case; inside and outside all that we see are pictures made of light.

I have written of some experiences I had of the type of thinking that I am advocating:

> In England. Today I walk in the rain of this December afternoon and I think of a mountain in Ceylon, the Mountain of Butterflies. As I climb, I imagine the butterflies, the dreams of Holy Men fluttering in a brilliant light. We are an irreligious people, we do not see the silver water balloons on the birch trees and the tall beech trees clothed in their green armour of lichens like prophets; we have no holy mountains nor holy rivers. But long ago before the Druids, the natives saw visions in these groves.
>
> The sun penetrates the mist and I find myself in a world of dazzling light and the rain running down the beeches is like a tide of green blood and fire, its waves sparkling in the sunlight. I shake a birch tree and the silver water balloons fall to the ground and shatter. We have as many lovely things here as on the Mountain of Butterflies but we lack only the vision to see them.
>
> (*Gardens of Meditation*)

We must learn to see in the most humdrum event the wonder of reality. I was waiting in a car at night in the rain of a city street. All at once I was struck by the appearance of raindrops running down the windows. They were like little rafts of coloured lights, rainbow-cargoed boats, bubbling and sparkling. My mood changed from boredom to delight.

The poet's vision can change sorrow to joy. Indeed there is little great poetry that has not come from the frost of sorrow. This is the supreme compensation that gives the creative person the ability to distil from the very substance of sorrow a beauty that transforms the world into paradise.

Those who suffer in life can take refuge in the transcendent ocean from where they are inspired and moved by the Eternal as if the flavour of that great ocean of light has entered them, so their speech has that same flavour.

What matters is not the object of sight but the poetic vision. Thus Ramakrishna, the Holy Man of Calcutta, saw Benares not as a material city but as the dreams and hopes of holy pilgrims that had fallen on the city, stratum on stratum, making it a city of holy ideas, a spiritual city.

In looking at buildings and cities in India it often appears to one that they are not physical cities at all; it is as if mystic plans by religious architects had been changed from dream-visions into physical cities.

Even in our materialistic West it is possible to see behind pictures the dream that has taken form in material and been framed and hung on a wall. A vision by a sculptor is solidified into a statue. Such visions are to be seen in all great art.

There are no mundane objects, everything is a sacred artifact. At the ordinary verbal level an object may seem commonplace but to the mystic it is lifted up and transfigured, a casting of the divine light. A Holy Man was approached by an aspirant to become a disciple. The young man was given the task of looking at a flower day after day, week after week. He suffered agonies of boredom till after many months he began to see it in a new way, as it really was, and discerned its subtle beauty.

It is easy to see beauty in a garden but what about seeing it in the cams and gears of industry? Here also the real can be seen. I have written about the two modes of thinking, but there is a third*, though it is really only a modification of the second. The first is ordinary Aristotelian Thinking, which is illusory in the sense of Plato's Cave where the shadows are mistaken for reality; it is also

---

There may be a fourth mode of thinking. The flower meditation described above is the deepest meditation of all. It is a state where the meditator coalesces with the object. He becomes the flower and enjoys a spiritual relationship with it. This makes use of the mysterious consciousness. It is a relationship we should have with all objects but especially our fellow beings. In this way instead of being isolated in the bunkers of our memory-dominated thought, we escape and see over the parapet described in the last pages of this book and become part of the Cosmos.

hopelessly inaccurate. The second is Non-Aristotelian Thinking done subconsciously as in a game of skill; it is accurate because we are not sidetracked by the red herrings of similarities and analogies. It sees what really is. The third is creative thought done in reveries and using meditation and intuition in which the Higher Intelligence or Nous is given full scope and there is ample time for the gestation of new ideas and creativity. It is the way geniuses think. This way can be applied even to the cams and gears mentioned at the beginning of the paragraph, for everything has a divine dimension.

Chapter 10
Poetry and Mysticism

I believe that creativity is the best means of reaching Realization, and of course poetry must be one of the most universal uses of creativity, which goes on to levels of higher poetry and mystical verse that are hardly dreamt of by those who teach creativity. Concerning the point about poetry being valuable for teaching Realization, it is of interest to know that the great 7th/8th-century sage Shankaracharya became Realized only after he wrote the sacred poem "Hymn to the Mother Goddess Annapurna".

By poetry I mean verse that is creative and concerns the Unspeakable regions beyond the gross senses; it has to lead to states of joy such as Creative Rapture and the Peak Experience, which are met when the mind throws off its shackles of words and soars into the transcendent.

Korzybski wrote of the distinction between the real world and the conditioned one that most people suppose is the real, by the analogy of a cinema film. Each frame is advanced a little over the one before it so that in running the film, an impression of life is given. If, however, each frame is removed and looked at individually, everything of the story and movement and emotion is lost. This is what people do in life: they take the world before them, which is moving and dynamic, and they place the little bits of it, the individual pictures and words, in storage in their minds. Eventually they become so enamoured of the static pictures that they impose them on reality so that the moving real is no more.

The principle in writing poetry is the same as for all creativity; the poet sees an event or object at a deep level using their Creative Intelligence, and as they look intently they gain feelings of rapture. They then translate their feelings into visual images and finally turn them into words. The reader of this poetry must translate the words into the original emotions of the poet or they will miss the whole meaning of the poem.

Images of poetry often come in reveries, which is exactly the same as in the creativity of scientists and inventors. Coleridge and Wordsworth used to go on long walks when some of their poetic images came to them.

Many ideas come in the hours of sleep, especially in the twilight world between waking and sleeping, and some ideas come in drugged states and under the influence of alcohol.

In his book *The Road to Xanadu* J. L. Lowes wrote about the creative process in the mind of Coleridge. Lowes undertook the task of searching into Coleridge's past reading to find where his poetic images came from. This was a stupendous task because Coleridge was a voluminous reader; however, he kept a list of the books he had read in a notebook, enabling Lowes to trace many of the images to their source.

Coleridge's mind took the raw material of poets and explorers and twisted it and mixed it with many other ideas to produce his poetry. The mind is like a vat in which time works on all ideas and changes them, producing creative images. After taking some opium prescribed for an ailment he had, Coleridge entered a reverie after reading Samuel Purchas's *Purchas His Pilgrim* (1613) where these words appear: "In Zamdu did Cublai Can build a stately Palace, encompassing sixteene miles of plaine ground with a wall, wherein are fertile Meddowes, Pleasant Springs, delightful Streames, and all sorts of beasts of chase and game, and in the midst thereof a sumptuous house of pleasure, which may be moved from place to place . . ."

Coleridge's poem Kubla Khan came from this origin. Here is the first verse:

> In Xanadu did Kubla Khan
> A stately pleasure-dome decree;
> Where Alph, the sacred river, ran
> Through caverns measureless to man
>   Down to a sunless sea.
> So twice five miles of fertile ground
> With walls and towers were girdled round:
> And there were gardens bright with sinuous rills,
> Where blossomed many an incense-bearing tree;

> And here were forests ancient as the hills,
> Enfolding sunny spots of greenery.

The beginning of the poem came from Purchas's images but they in turn roused other images from his past reading. For instance, some of the images came from Milton's *Paradise Lost*, some came from James Bruce's account of the source and fountains of the Blue Nile in Abyssinia, whence also came the Abyssinian maid playing on her dulcimer. The Milk of Paradise came from the story of the Old Man of the Mountains, Hassan, who drugged men and sent them forth as Assassins. Some of the images were traced to an author's account of Kashmir, and some to another one of Florida by a different author. All these images were changed and combined by the creative process of Coleridge's mind into the superb poem. Many of his images came from accounts of explorers that were the rage at that time, in fact much of the *The Rime of the Ancient Mariner* came from accounts of the sea voyages of discovery.

To learn about poetic creativity H. D. Thoreau is an ideal person to study because he used metaphor frequently – indeed he has been described as having developed a metaphorical form of writing. Here is an example of his style, which is in agreement with Synectics' teaching. He wrote of waking to a morning of joy:

> Those undescribed, ambrosial mornings of summer which I can remember when a thousand birds were heard gently twittering and ushering in the light, like the argument to a new canto of an epic and heroic poem. The serenity, the infinite promise of such a morning. The song or twitter of the birds drips from the leaves like dew. Then there was something divine and immortal in our life. When I have waked up on my couch in the woods and seen the day dawning, and heard the twitter of the birds.

He wrote poetry and prose but his best work was prose written in his *Journal*. He lived alone, alienated from humanity of his time who were materialists and could never understand his writings. In a passage, which is valuable for its insight into Realization, he castigated scientists who were then largely non-creative, their task being to gain a comfortable and conventional explanation for every puzzling phenomenon brought to their notice. In contrast, present-day physicists and biologists are working at the frontiers of science, where they are finding that spirit and matter are converging and ideas such as the morphogenetic field, string theory and black holes are gaining credibility; these ideas, even if they had been discovered in Thoreau's day, would not have been countenanced. Thoreau commented:

> It is only when we forget all our learning that we begin to know. I do not get nearer by a hair's breadth to any natural object so long as I presume that I have to have an introduction to it from some learned man. To conceive of it with a total apprehension, I must for the thousandth time approach it as something totally strange. If you would make acquaintance with the ferns, you must forget your botany. You must get rid of what is commonly called KNOWLEDGE of them. Not a single scientific term or distinction is the least to the purpose, for you would fain perceive something and you must approach the object totally unprejudiced. You must be aware that NO THING is what you have taken it to be. In what book is this world and its beauty described? You have to be in a different state from common. Your greatest success will be simply to perceive that such things are, and you will have no communication to make to the Royal Society. If it were required to know the position of the fruit dots or the character of the indusium, nothing could be easier than to ascertain it; but if it is required that you be affected by ferns, that they amount to anything to you, that they be another sacred scripture and revelation to you, helping to redeem your life, this is not so surely accomplished.
>
> *(Journal*, Oct. 4, 1859)

Of the first way he wrote: "This is the Chinese, the Aristotelian method."

Baudelaire wrote a poem about an albatross caught on the deck of a ship where it was mocked by sailors for its ungainliness, its great wings an encumbrance to it. He suggested that the same encumbrance hampered poets, their giant wings a hindrance in the everyday world. But this is a Western idea exemplifying tortured poets such as François Villon, Rimbaud and Dylan Thomas. In the East poets are often Realized beings who are full of joy and they sense their indestructible oneness with all things, they are philosopher-poets.

A deeper kind of poetry that is hardly understood in the West is about seeing beyond the senses. Much of it comes from Persia, a country of supreme poets. In ordinary poetry, the poet writes about the Unspeakable but retains a footing in the physical world; in contrast, in mystic poetry the poet enters the Unspeakable in states of ecstasy and trance and writes of their experiences in that vast region.

Persian and Arab poets call it the Unseen World; other names for it are Placelessness and Spacelessness. In sleep, which for mystics is a time of the greatest joy, they leave the world of verbal conditioning and enter the trackless paths of the spiritual world.

The greatest Persian mystic poet Jalaluddin Rumi wrote in his *Mathnawi*:

> The Saints and Prophets are explorers of the Unseen World. First they journeyed to the other world, coming out of their human attributes the flesh and the skin. They surveyed the depths and heights of that world and this, and traversed all the stages so that it became known to them how one must proceed on that way. Then they came back and summoned mankind saying, "Come to that original world for this world is a ruin and a perishing abode, and we have discovered a delightful place of which we tell you".

All mystics know of the limitation of words. Sana i, poet of Ghazna and preceptor of Rumi, wrote: "What is reason in this Guest House [the world]? Only a crooked writer of the script of God." He knew the gap that exists between words and the real, the script of God. He wrote of the world beyond the senses: "In the realm of the soul are skies lording over the sky of this world. In the way of the spirit there are lowlands and highlands, there are lofty mountains and seas."

Rumi commented on this couplet: "The Unseen World has other clouds and water than ours, it has another sky and sun that is not discerned except by the Elect."

Sana i wrote about how to read the Koran in his *Enclosed Garden of the Truth*: "How shalt thou taste the flavour and delight of the Koran, since thou chantest it without comprehension? Come forth through the door of the body into the landscape of the soul: come and view the contents of the Koran, that all things may appear before thy soul ... The contents of the Koran are scattered pearls."

Nous is the key to this door of the body. Korzybski's Unspeakable makes sense of these mystic ideas; the wonderlands of mystic poetry are not then some wild phantasmagoria of deranged minds but a subtle reality. Rumi wrote: "If you pass beyond forms, O friends, it's paradise and rose gardens within rose gardens." He meant by forms the outside of things, our conditioned view of reality that must be transcended.

Ramakrishna, the Sage of Calcutta, told a story of a disciple asking a Holy Man about the spiritual journey. He was told to "Go Farther!" So he went farther into the forest and came upon a grove of Sandalwood trees, which he harvested. On returning to the Holy Man he was told again: "Go Farther!" He passed the sandalwood trees and came upon a gold mine. Later still he was told: "Go Farther!", when he reached emerald mines and became extremely rich. This is the spiritual journey.

There is no end to the joys and riches of the spiritual journey.

The seeing of reality is taught in all higher religions, which speak of the immanence of the Divine in all things so that the whole universe and everything in it is the Divine, and even the most insignificant object is suffused with the Divine Principle. Sri Krishna Prem (Ronald Nixon), a university professor who had been a British fighter pilot in the First World War, later becoming a Sannyasi in the Himalayas, wrote of this and how the mind must learn to see the Divine in all things using the Higher Intelligence:

> Each being on Earth is a reflection of an aspect of Atman (Universal Spirit or Divine). This reflection is best seen in those objects that are pre-eminent in their class; for it is in them that the Divine Archetype has found most expression. In all things HE is to be sought. "What makes the Gods shining and powerful? It is the Light and Power of the One. What is it that calls forth our aspirations in the sight of mountain peaks, calms us in sheets of water, whispers to us in trees, disturbs our hearts in animals or thrills in gleaming weapons? What is it but HIM shining through all these

beings, in spiritual powers to which if we give names they are but poor translations for our weakness." "We must not turn from these perceptions as mere fancies, … what is thus felt in beings is not fancy but something truly, if but vaguely, seen within. The disciple must cling to these intuitive perceptions and sharpen them to clearness until the outer forms become unreal things through whose translucid shells the wondrous powers shine in their gleaming splendours."

(from *The Yoga of the Kathopanishad*)

As soon as we can see reality as it is, the world becomes transformed into beauty; moreover, anyone who can understand mystic poetry will understand Non-Aristotelian Thinking. I spoke with my friend Krishna Khosla, the author of *The Sufism of Rumi*, who knew more about mystic poetry than anyone else I have met, and when I showed him a description of Non-Aristotelian Thinking, he understood it immediately because it is the same kind of thinking.

Non-Aristotelian Thinking is part of all higher religion because the words of Holy Men have to be translated into the language of the soul. All books of higher religion are only maps of the mystic world and the individual soul has to make the journey into the territory alone. Most people never understand this and it entails great effort to make the journey, so it is only when a crisis arises in a person's life, and they realise that the way they live and all their values have no meaning, that they may be spurred to make the mental journey. Coming out of their disillusionment and despondency, they will learn of another way of living that is far more rewarding and fulfilling than the materialistic life they have lived up to that time. They turn inward and instead of reacting to events they use their Higher Intelligence.

Within the self they will search for the Divine, which is seen as the Universal Light of Consciousness; this is the only part of them that is eternal, all the rest must perish. Everything they do and all their problems from that time on are referred to the higher consciousness and this gives serenity and joy because they are no longer caught up in the frantic material world but have become a dweller in the Eternal. This person is no dried-up ascetic, which is abhorrent to most sane people, but inside them is a fountain of joy that can never fail.

Mysticism is a higher religion that has nothing in it about rules, dogma or ritual. It is seen in its noblest writing, a sublime poetry. The aspirant who reads it must be moved in their soul; ultimately, if they persist they will experience states of delight and Release, which have such names as grace, *moksa*, heaven, nirvana and *satori*. None of these can be reached by verbal logic but using Non-Aristotelian Thinking they are open to every seeker.

An idea of mysticism in the Middle East and Europe is the Orient – a world separate from our mundane world, which has nothing to do with our geography books. It originated with the Christian Gnostics and was celebrated in the *Hymn of the Soul* that is also called the *Song of the Pearl*:

> A young prince was sent from the Orient, the spiritual world, to Egypt, the material world, by his parents to bring back the Pearl without price. He arrives in the land of Egypt, he is fed the food of forgetfulness. He receives a message from his father and his mother, the Queen of the Orient. This causes him to remember his origin and the mission he has to accomplish and who he is. He returns to the Orient.
>
> (From the Acts of St. Thomas)

This story is about our origin in the Orient and how we forget it when we are born. Few people ever remember their origin, yet we are all of the Orient. The mystic poet, however, does remember and enters the Orient. They are calm, free, no longer entangled in the material world.

The worst illusion of all that human beings suffer is the name we receive at birth. We are saddled with it like a beast of burden, but unlike the beast of burden we are never unloaded. Some religious groups who see this danger give their members new names but these are also labels; for most of these people it amounts only to a change of burden. There is a story in mysticism of a woman whose name was Banafshi (Violet) but she had an esoteric name, Istaftin, of the spiritual world, a name in heaven. This reminds us of our real name of the Orient, our secret meditative name. The ordinary human name, even if it was not an illusion, can refer only to the material being, whereas the real being is the Higher Consciousness or Nous. This is the entity that needs an esoteric or visionary name.

When the poet enters their mind there is not just darkness. It is the pool of light, the luminous sea of mysticism. Nights especially are the poet's joy; they return from them with mystic gifts, ephemeral flowers of the darkness that must be written down at once, for like fairy flowers they die as soon as they are picked.

A mystic sees a deeper beauty, whereas the ordinary materialist sees only a fraction of reality, the rest masked by memory and words. Objects have been called "Pictures made of Light" by Nisargadatta Maharaj, an idea endorsed by the physicist David Bohm who described them as a kind of condensed or frozen light. We have made our minds into Towers of Babel: we should turn them into galleries of pictures.

Mystic poetry is a mixture of transcendent poetry, philosophy and mystic religion. In a story of Rumi, a mystic was looking at an orchard of trees whose fruit was so abundant that the leaves could not be seen. Nearby in the desert were thousands of people walking on the burning sand, desperate for shade and water. The mystic Daquqi spoke to them, urging them to slake their thirst with the fruit. But they all said he was mad. He went up to the trees and savoured their fruit.

This is the spiritual orchard that is never seen by most people and even the greatest poets have been unable to make them see it. Yet it is one of the supreme delights of life and it is waiting for every aspirant.

The main purpose of this book has been to teach Non-Aristotelian Thinking, which is the same kind of thinking as that used in mystic poetry. Non-Aristotelian Thinking is about the limitation of words and memory, just like poetry, whose beauty of is forever beyond words. It appears to be written in words of our language but the words are transcendent and refer to an unknown landscape in an unknown language. It can be thought of as an exploration of a terra incognita, a mystic Antarctica, where nothing of our mundane world applies. In this it is no different from approaching quantum physics, which bears little relation to our ordinary world. We have to come to mystic writing in the same state of deliberate forgetfulness and suspended judgement, using only perception including intuition, visualisation and imagination.

My idea of mysticism is of a higher poetry in which logic and rationality are unimportant. What is important is that we sense the beauty, the theophanic beauty of it. We have to be moved by it and sense rapture and delight. The utmost beauty is marked by tears. "Recognise the travellers on the path of his love by their pallid cheeks. Know that the pearls of love are tears" (Rumi, *Mathnawi*).

Sufis say that the stains of the soul will be expunged only by the water of the eyes. Your heart must melt in love, and your eyes become two rivers if you aspire to the other world. Rumi compared tears and the effect they have on the soul to drops of rain on the desert. One of these drops will become a pearl, another a narcissus.

Tears rank higher than the blood of martyrs in mysticism.

The idea of the Orient has inspired even Western poets. One of these was Gerard de Nerval (1808–55) who, when asked after a party if he wanted to be taken home, declined saying that he was going to the Orient. In a passage that recalls Rumi's nights of joy and many descriptions in the writings of such mystics as Yahya Suhrawardi, he wrote:

> So we ascended during the night and were forced to descend again during the day.... It was like a primitive and celestial family, whose smiling eyes sought mine with sweet compassion. There I felt bitterly that I was only a momentary sojourner in that world, that foreign yet cherished world, and I trembled at the thought that I must return and re-enter life. In vain did women and children crowd about me as if to hold me back. Already their nascent forms were dissolving in confused vapours; the fair faces paled, and the clear features, the sparkling eyes were lost in darkness in which the last radiance of a smile still shone.

Chapter 11
Letting Go and Just Being:
A Way of Release

Nisargadatta Maharaj was a teacher in Bombay who gained a large following of Indians and Westerners. He spoke to his followers like this:

> Can you sit on the floor? Do you need a cushion? Have you any questions to ask? Not that you need ask anything. Such an apparently lazy way of spending time is highly regarded in India. It means that for the time being you are free from the obsession with "what to do next". When you are not in a hurry and the mind is free of anxiety, it becomes quiet and in the silence something may be heard that is ordinarily too fine and subtle for perception. The mind must be open and quiet to see. What we are doing here is to bring our minds into the right state for understanding what is real.

Much of our thinking is sub-conscious, which is to be seen most obviously in games of skill and such activities as typing or driving a car where we have to learn appropriate reflex actions. Verbal learning of such skills gives no proficiency; we have to practise them in order to become experts. Eugen Herrigel's *Zen in the Art of Archery* demonstrated this by showing how in the end the Master Archer shoots without conscious thought.

Life should be lived in the same way. When we live verbally and consciously, we supervise ourselves and life is lived in a strait-jacket. We must practise and learn to 'Just Be', trusting our sub-conscious intelligence or Nous. Someone who does this will find that they perform better, because instead of being concerned with what they are going to say or do, they are 'Just Being', giving no thought to what words will come out or what they will do; they becomes absolutely free and natural. We give no thought to our bodily functions such as breathing and digestion; in the same way we should give no thought to our external actions in life. Such a person who is 'Just Being' is released: they become free and a burden is lifted from their back. This same freedom is discussed later in this book in Chapter 12, "Philosophy of Freedom".

The non-verbal thinking of Nous is an anodyne against despair and sorrow. At the thought of the word 'death' dark fears can arise, but as soon as the mind is changed to Nous they recede because Nous is about the here and now; it doesn't allow the present to be contaminated by thoughts of the past or the future, it insulates the being from the tyranny of time and death and fear. It places us in the 'Here Now', which is the only reality; yesterday and tomorrow are man-made verbal abstractions and not real. For many people the living of one day at a time, ignoring past and future, gives tranquillity and assurance. Even the most unhappy and desperate person can survive a day – they have only to live till nightfall.

'Just Being' has many virtues; one of these is to fight phobias, many of which are brought on by excessive thought. In this category come fears such as a sense of inadequacy, fear of flying and many others. 'Just Being' without verbal thinking can help to alleviate them and eventually overcome them. It is often fear coming from thought in words that inhibits. Once the way of living without words is mastered by practice, it is as if such problems melt away; they become unimportant and you give no thought to them but 'Just Be': you 'Let Go!'

In fact 'Just Being' without verbal thought is your demonstrating who and what you really are. Most people's behaviour is a facade; they are thinking all the time what they are going to say or do, in other words acting instead of just being what they really are. Life has to be lived spontaneously, not in a calculated fashion. This means avoiding all artificiality, otherwise you are not being 'you', you have presented your deputy to the world. The only people who are truly themselves are young children before their schooling and the adult world afflict them and destroy their happiness. Too soon they start to live the second-handed life of adults.

With practice the Nous mode of thought can become habitual. It can be trusted implicitly because it is a tapping into an intelligence far larger and more resourceful than ordinary rational intelligence.

Though Nous is the secret of creativity and all higher abilities of the mind such as vision, it must not be used exclusively. The two modes of thought complement each other. Creative ideas from

Nous must be checked and corroborated by the rational mind. The two modes can be thought of as acting alternately; together they expand our capability immeasurably and give us a vastly enhanced potential. However, the rational mode should be confined to its subordinate role.

'Letting Go' and 'Just Being' are primarily about Freedom or Release, which is the most important aim of Eastern religions. This idea of Freedom or Liberation as a direct aim of life is practically universal in all Far Eastern countries. One of the necessities for achieving this aim is to overcome one's desires, which are the chief hindrance on the spiritual path. Stoic philosophy has the same rule about desires; for instance, Seneca wrote of hope and fear following in each others' footsteps like the guard and the prisoner.

Underlying the idea of 'Just Being' should be a lifelong purpose. Just as purpose is a vital need for all human endeavour including the running of companies, an aspirant on the road of life must have a purpose. But the human purpose for a life time is not so easy to formulate as for companies with their relatively short time horizons. As the person progresses in life, they have to revise their purpose as they move forward. Above all it must have no end. It is not advisable to have a finite goal for when that is reached the person will enter a vacuum; indeed there can be no end to the possible spiritual aims of a human being.

I think of this book as being a guide for an aspirant. At first they have the basic needs, as set out by Maslow, to fulfil or sublimate using philosophy or religion, etc. They can then move to higher needs such as self-fulfilment leading to creativity. Then may come the seeing of reality, and finally the aim of Freedom and Liberation discussed in the last chapters of this book.

Steady progress gives assurance so that even during the struggles of life, the aspirant will always sense that there is more to it than the mere scratching a living. Moreover, it will throw their material successes and failures into perspective. All that is really important is that they sense that they progress in the living of life and that they are growing in stature; furthermore, the self-assurance gained will help in the material life for they will be seeing things more accurately and will not be agitated by hope and fear – it confers tranquillity.

Rabindranath Tagore wrote of Indian peasants who have seen through the illusion of life: they can teach us what is really important. Here are his words about those rare spirits who set out in search of Freedom (*mukti, moksa,* Liberation).

> They are unconcerned about success or security but are afraid of being alienated from the world of truth, afraid of perpetual drifting amidst the froth and foam of things, of being tossed about by the tidal waves of pleasure and pain and never reaching the ultimate meaning of life.
>
> And they have seen men who are not above their own level in social position or intellectual acquirement, going out to seek truth, leaving everything that they have behind them. They know that the object of these adventures is not betterment in worldly wealth and power – it is freedom – release. They possibly know some poor fellow villager of their own craft, who remained in the world, carrying on his daily vocation yet has the reputation of being emancipated in the heart of the Eternal.
>
> I myself have come across a fisherman singing with an inward absorption of mind while fishing in the Ganges. He was pointed out to me by my boatman with awe, as a man of liberated spirit. He is out of reach of the conventional prices set upon men by society, and which classify them like toys arranged in the shop windows according to their market standard of value.
>
> When the figure of this fisherman comes to my mind, I cannot but think that their number is not small who with their lives sing the epic of the unfettered soul, but will never be known in history. These unsophisticated Indian peasants know that an emperor is merely a decorated slave remaining chained to his empire, that a millionaire is kept pilloried by his fate in the golden cage of his wealth, while this fisherman is free in the realms of light.
>
> (R. Tagore, *The Religion of Man*)

The fisherman shows that these people do not have to abandon all, but can continue with their occupation. And let us not look down on these people with scorn from the vantage point of our vaunted education. It is instructional to know that the greatest prophets and seers were largely illiterate and in our sense ignorant people.

Sri Aurobindo, Seer of Pondicherry, who had been a distinguished scholar at Oxford, wrote of the Veda, whose authors we would now presumably scorn as ignorant savages:

> The sacred poems . . . are among the most beautiful, solemn and profound that the imagination of man has conceived. The Adityas (Sons of the Infinite–Varuna, Mitra and Aryaman) are described in formulas of an incomparable grandeur and sublimity. No mythic barbarian gods of cloud, sun and shower are these, no confused allegories of wonder-stricken savages, but the objects of worship to men far more inwardly civilised and profound than ourselves ...
>
> *(On the Veda, p. 546)*

Tagore wrote a poem about the joy of life that is derived from Freedom:

> On the day when the Lotus bloomed, my mind was straying and I knew it not. Only now and again a sadness fell upon me, and I started up from my dream and I felt a sweet trace of a strange fragrance in the south wind. That vague sweetness made my heart ache with longing and it seemed to me that it was the eager breath of the summer seeking its completion. I knew not then that it was so near, that it was mine, and that this perfect sweetness had blossomed in my own heart.

This sweetness can arise even in the work-a-day world when the mind turns to mysticism; it is like the fragrance of distant orange groves, bringing a feeling of relief and certainty and inexpressible wellbeing. It is the perpetual dawns written about in the Vedas, when one dawn follows another so swiftly that they become perpetual. It is a rebirth of the soul into a new region of light and air after the dungeons of material life. It is the sorrowless land of Kabir the Weaver, where the unstruck music sounds.

Release comes at the moment when the mind believes in the unseen world; until that moment it is only an intellectual understanding of it, but when there is certainty, not of the mind alone but of all the fibres of the body, then the idea dawns like a new sun and there arises the sweet feeling of delight and relief. The physical world becomes like a dream and we look at it half smilingly, knowing that we will never again be enthralled by it. Then comes the supreme sweetness and the scent of the Eternal and we are overwhelmed with the sense of having discarded our shackles and that we are forever free.

Chapter 12
Philosophy of Freedom

I wrote elsewhere of Ancient Wisdom, referring to religion. I shall use the same expression for philosophy, calling it Ancient Philosophy. I mean by this the love of wisdom, which is epitomised in Plato: "Philosophy is learning how to die, then you know how to live." These were not mere words, for Socrates in his noble death, described by Plato, taught how a man should live and die. People in the West are not taught Ancient Philosophy so they are cast adrift without rudders in mountainous seas.

Philosophy in the West departed from Ancient Philosophy and entered the pursuit of knowledge and understanding. I recall an example of this from the philosopher A. J. Ayer about what we see when we look at a penny coin. I have never regarded such information as much use in the storms of life. Ancient Philosophy is seen in the writings of Stoic philosophers such as Epictetus and Seneca. The famous scholar Lipsius wrote: "When I read Seneca, I think I am beyond human fortunes on the top of a hill overlooking mortality."

What these philosophers taught was what we have under our control, that is what we think about things. Everything else is outside our control. Stronger men in greater numbers can thwart all our aims, hence it can all be ignored because there is nothing we can ultimately do about it. In every situation we have only to do our best, that is behave well, have courage, kindness and decency, in short behave like the best of mankind. "And what if I do the opposite, what if I lie and cheat and steal, what injury will I do myself?" To this question Epictetus replied: "No injury but that of not doing what you ought. You will destroy the man of fidelity in you, the man of honour, the man of decent behaviour. You need not look for greater injuries than these."

Socrates rejoiced for a similar reason: "Is it nothing in your eyes never to bring accusation against anyone, never to blame anyone, always to wear the same expression on your face?"

Philosophy gives a person armour and weapons for life and it civilises its devotees.

Epictetus taught that the greater the challenge, the greater the glory to be gained from facing it fearlessly. He called this the magic wand of philosophy: "Bring what you will and with a wave of my wand, I will turn it to good. The bad neighbour is bad for himself but for me he is good because he exercises my kindness and fairness and my good disposition." "Bring me death and like Socrates, I will turn it into my everlasting glory."

And what of the ridiculous disputes you see nowadays between neighbours over something as trivial as a boundary hedge? Some people spend a lifetime over such a dispute and lose a fortune in litigation. This can be contrasted with Epictetus; when he was arguing with a rich man, someone said to him, "If I devote myself to philosophy, I shall not own a farm, or have riches or own silver goblets and gold plate." Epictetus replied:

> To all this it is perhaps enough to answer "I do not need them". But you, even if you acquire many possessions, need still others and whether you will or not, are more poverty stricken than I am. What then do I need? What you do not have; steadfastness, your mind in a state of conformity with nature, freedom from vexation of spirit. I am richer than you are; all this is an offset to your silver plate and your gold plate. You have furnishings of gold, but your reason, your judgement, your assent, your choice, your desire of earthenware; everything you already have seems small in your sight, but everything I have seems important to me. Your strong desire is insatiate, mine is already satisfied. For you will learn that none of these things, which are admired and sought after ... are of any good to those who attain them – for when they do get them, the burning heat is just as bad, there is the same tossing about on the sea, the same desire for what they do not have. For freedom is not acquired by satisfying yourself with what you desire, but by destroying your desire.

In addition to the Stoics' teaching of how human beings should behave and live, an even more ancient philosophy taught creativity. In a book by Peter Kingsley called *In the Dark Places of Wisdom*, he used archaeological finds, in particular those at Elea (or its other name, Velia) where Parmenides was born and taught, to guide his researches.

Parmenides, as Plato spelt it, was the main character in the dialogue of the same name. 'Parmeneides' with the additional 'e' was written on a statue to him, found at Velia. Wording on the statue described him as a physician but of the whole being, not a mere doctor. He was also a lawgiver, prophet and poet.

It was the practice for initiates to enter caves where they were guided by leaders. 'Incubation' took place and they went into different states of consciousness. They were described as being of another world. They were taught to see reality: they became Realized beings. This was in stark contrast to ordinary people described by Parmeneides:

> For helplessness in their chests is what steers their wandering minds as they are carried along in a daze, deaf and blind at the same time, indistinguishable, undistinguishing crowds.

The Naasene Document records what the initiate eventually becomes:

> The Phrygians call him (man) also Dead, when buried in the body as in a tomb or sepulchre ... The same Phrygians again call the very same man after the transformation God or a God ...

The followers of Parmeneides and, it must be added, generations of predecessors of his, were taught not only to see reality, but lawgiving, healing of the whole man, prophecy, poetry, dying before dying as in many religions including Christianity and Islam, and other subjects.

Healing implied finding out what you are behind the world of senses, i.e. what you really are. Other forms of consciousness and other worlds were entered in ecstasies, dreams and reveries. In the caves where 'incubation' took place, the initiates had to be silent and still. Silence and stillness were of the essence.

In this silence a piping sound was heard from the syrinx, a musical instrument or part of a musical instrument. It is a hissing that is commonly heard in meditation and 'incubation' indicating that the initiate is nearing their goal. The Indian kundalini or serpent power is the same.

It is very clear that at the root of all this creativity was what we call Non-Aristotelian Thinking; that is intuitive, creative and visual thought. Verbal logic by comparison is sterile and barren. How the West changed from such creative and dynamic thinking to verbal logic is one of the mysteries of Western Philosophy.*

Philosophy gives perspective and puts material things in their place. A poet, Sadi, wrote of a merchant who was with a group in a bazaar telling them tales. The merchant said to them that he was in the desert and all his provisions were consumed and he was preparing to die. At that moment he saw a bag of pearls. "Never shall I forget the joy I felt, deeming them to be parched grain, nor the bitterness and despair when I found them to be pearls."

No finer statement has ever been made about why we should think well of our fellow beings than this episode in the life of Jalaluddin Rumi. He was told that another Sufi master always spoke of him with the utmost admiration. Rumi said:

> If any man speaks well of another, that good appraisal reverts again to himself and in reality it is himself that he is praising and applauding. It is like a man who sows round his house flowers and aromatic herbs; whenever he looks out, he sees flowers and aromatic herbs and is always in Paradise, inasmuch as he has formed the habit of speaking well of other men. Whenever a man has engaged himself in speaking well of another, that person becomes his friend;

I have never been enamoured of Western philosophers with certain exceptions, such as the Stoics and some passages of Plato, notably on Socrates' death and some others, and Kant, Hume, Nietzsche, Schopenhauer. Immediately words in the form of close reasoning, such as dialectic, appeared, my eyes seemed to glaze over. If the words did not refer to something tangible or to some feeling, they were for me meaningless. And the whole great edifice of words – a mere house of cards. I compared this with the simple method of science, that is checking everything against reality. Like China, we were held back by verbal reasoning for thousands of years. In contrast to dialectic, Parmeneides' meditational philosophy actually leads to something: poetry, lawgiving, healing etc., hence for me it is valid and useful.

when he remembers him, he brings to mind a friend, and bringing to mind a friend is like flowers and a flower-garden, it is refreshment and repose. But when a man speaks ill of another, that person becomes hateful in his eyes; whenever he remembers him and his image comes before him, it is as though a snake or a scorpion, a thorn or a thistle has appeared in his sight.

(Arberry, *Discourses of Rumi*)

Nothing is more sure than this, that if we speak and think well of other people it makes life more joyful, but if we think ill of them we turn our lives into a battlefield.

Our using philosophy does not mean that we become ineffectual people blown about by the winds of material life. On the contrary we shall be more effective, because we shall see reality more accurately so that we shall not be swayed by hope and fear, the two scourges of the mind mentioned by Seneca that follow one another like the guard and the prisoner.

Epictetus looked at all events from a higher viewpoint. It is a matter of perspective. A riot in a ghetto of a city may be terrible for the ghetto dwellers. For the mayor of that city it is less terrible but it is still sufficiently near to them to be a serious worry. At the higher level of the Governor of the state to which that city belongs, the riot will be regarded only as a nuisance; above that, to the Monarch or Premier of the country it will hardly matter and to the world as a whole it will be trivial.

Even more insulation is given by looking at all things from the transcendent of the spiritual world, for then each event appears as through coloured lenses that transform it and place it in another dimension and time. Epictetus's magic wand can make all things, including poverty, to be of no account; mystic poetry goes beyond negation and writes of a rare beauty to be found in misfortune and poverty.

In the West we have lost most criteria of worth other than money and intellectual attainment, but in the East the highest aim has always been Release, Liberation or Freedom. It does not matter how poor or base in origin a person is, attainment of Freedom gives them a stature beyond wealth. Such a person was Raidas the

Sweeper, who will be remembered in India for ever. A sweeper is the lowest of the low in the caste system of India. Tagore wrote a poem about this rare spirit:

> Raidas, the sweeper, sat still, lost in the solitude of his soul, and some songs born of his silent vision found their way to the Rani's heart – the Rani Jhali of Chittore. Tears flowed from her eyes, her thoughts wandered away from her daily duties, till she met Raidas who guided her to God's presence.
>
> The old Brahmin priest of the King's house rebuked her for her desecration of sacred law by offering homage as a disciple to an outcaste.
>
> "Brahmin," the Rani answered, "while you were busy tying your purse-strings of custom ever tighter, love's gold slipped unnoticed to the earth and my Master in his divine humility has picked it up from the dust. Revel in your pride of the unmeaning knots without number, harden your miserly heart, but I, a beggar woman, am glad to receive love's wealth, the gift of the lowly dust, from my Master, the sweeper."
>
> (*Collected Poems and Plays*)

Hindus, Tibetan Buddhists and Zen Buddhists teach Release directly, which is entirely rational. It is not a typically Western idea of religion such as faith. Korzybski did not teach Freedom or Release, yet his teaching is almost the same as Zen, that is the illusory and pernicious influence of words. Through Nous or Non-Aristotelian Thinking we can reach the same freedom. As was written in the chapter "Letting Go and Just Being", we should give no thought to what we say or do but rely on our sub-conscious intelligence.

In Buddhism there are numerous stories about the same 'Letting Go' of rationality. It is verbal rationality that forms the chains that bind us. Ordinary human existence is likened to people clinging desperately to a small tree overhanging a chasm. All we have to do is 'Let Go!' The sub-conscious intelligence will act as a parachute, and we will be free. Very simple!

All Realized people say how simple it is; only the 'Letting Go' is the stumbling block. It takes courage to 'Let Go!'

Freedom is like happiness in that it cannot be approached directly. The desire for happiness or freedom prevents happiness. This is called seeking the fruit, whereas it is the action that is important. Desire in any form is death to happiness and freedom. Vinoba Bhave, a disciple of Gandhi who started the Bhoodan movement in India by which rich Indians donated land to the poor, wrote of this in a commentary on the *Bhagavadgita*:

> The noblest fruit of life is Freedom. But even for that Freedom we should not be greedy. That state will come to us unawares of its own accord. ... Therefore give up all thought of Freedom. The lover ... the Devotee of God however keeps saying to the Lord, "It is enough to love you, I do not want the fruit of Freedom (moksa)". After all, Freedom is also a kind of enjoyment, a kind of fruit... .
>
> By forgetting all about Freedom, one's efforts become more noble. Then Freedom will be enamoured of you. ... Round the neck of the seeker who without desire for Freedom is absorbed in devoted service, in effort, Moksa Lakshmi, the Goddess of Freedom, will throw the garland of victory.

(talks on the *Gita*, given by Vinoba Bhave to his fellow political prisoners of the British)

Chapter 13
The 'I' or Ego: *Know Thyself*

Complementary to philosophical ideas of the East is a system of the West that is particularly applicable to our modern world of pressures, deadlines, media and careers. It came from Carl Jung's book *Psychological Types*. It was the work of two people, Myers and Briggs, and it is called the Myers-Briggs Type Indicator. It is a method of making ourselves aware of the kind of people we are so that we do not live the lie of imitating others who are fundamentally different from ourselves. In this it is not very different from the Oriental aim of following one's *dharma*, meaning being what we are. It also helps to demonstrate the large differences between people, which makes it particularly valuable for counsellors and others who have to deal with people. Here I shall give the general outline of the principles, which should enable readers to get some idea of the kind of people they are. Later they may like to go further into the literature on the subject.

The Myers-Briggs Type Indicator (MBTI) (Rowan Bayne)

OPPOSITES

Attitude

E. Extravert: Gregarious, prefers outer world of people and things, active, gains energy from others. Uses experience, trial and error. Likes variety. Has social skills. Verbal.

I. Introvert: Prefers reflection and inner world, writing to talking. Quiet, reserved.

Function

S. Sensing: Likes facts, realistic, practical, observant, patient, good with detail, verbal thinker.

N. Intuitive: Imaginative, sees overall picture, works in bursts. Strategist.

Function

T. Thinking: Fair, firm minded, sceptical, logical, brisk, businesslike. Clear definitions and principles.

F. Feeling: Warm, sympathetic, has empathy with others. Likes harmony, clear values, is cheerful.

Attitude

J. Judging: Decisive, industrious, determined. Organised and systematic. Deadlines important. Likes things decided and settled. Good planner.

P. Perceiving: Curious, flexible and tolerant. Tends to leave things to last minute, impulsive.

Comments on the 16 types:

They should not be taken too literally but are given as a guide. It should be borne in mind that the individual attitudes and functions play a part in the full type description:

ISTJ   Many managers and accountants. Honour important to them. Thorough but may be thought inflexible.

ISFJ   Good with detail, very dependable.

INFJ   Some similarities with INFP.

INTJ   Look to future more than present, tough managers.

ISTP   Fond of sports, outdoors. Tend to be in job such as police officer but not detective.

ISFP   Like freedom to do what they want.

INFP   Tend to daydream. Have warm human values. Some are superactive.

INTP   Seek authority; intelligence important to them.

ESTP   Practical, prefer doing to study.

ESFP   Enjoy the good things of life – food, dress etc.

ENFP   Enthusiastic, versatile, lively, many are counsellors.

ENTP   Adaptable, innovative. Like work such as voluntary work abroad.

ESTJ   Organised. Seek work in management, police, etc.

ESFJ   Loyal to persons and organisations.

ENFJ   Similar to ESFJ.

ENTJ   Tough managers and executives.

All types can be found in all occupations but there are some types that tend to enter certain occupations:

SP   Performers, entrepreneurs, troubleshooters, one-person business owners.

SJ   Managers, accountants, police, dentists, teachers.

NT   Scientists, architects, engineers, designers, managers.

NF   Counsellors, journalists, artists, psychologists, clergy.

The way to ascertain one's type is as follows.

In the four letter types one of the central is the dominant, i.e. S, N, T, or F. The dominant one is the essential part of a person, with which they are most comfortable. For an extravert, this will be used in the outside world and for the introvert, the inside world. So there are eight possible combinations: ES, EN, ET, EF for extraverts and IS, IN, IT, IF for introverts.

The next important element to ascertain is that one opposite to the dominant, which will be the least used and therefore the one that we may do less well, leading to possible tension; it is the fourth function.

The next most important is the one beside the dominant in the middle two letters, which is the second in command or auxiliary. The other one is its partner, the third function. For instance in the type INTJ, N or T have to be the dominant ones. If it is N then T is the auxiliary; and the opposite of N, that is S, is the fourth or weakest function and the remaining letter, J, is the third function.

Both the dominant and the auxiliary should be reasonably well developed. It is advisable to get one's type checked by a person who knows one well; the opinion of a spouse or close friend can be invaluable.

Having read Rowan Bayne's book *Myers-Briggs Type Indicator*, I felt compelled to read Jung's *Psychological Types* from which the MBTI was derived. What I found particularly interesting about Jung's book were three features that were relevant to my own philosophical aims. They were:

1. The importance of developing all the psychological factors, not just the dominant and more obvious ones.

2. The decisive influence of introverted and extraverted thinking on human understanding.

3. Happiness and the existence of evil in the mind.

1. To succeed materially in life and make one's way, the dominant factors must be developed, but for the full participation in the whole of life the other factors must be nurtured. It was the German poet Schiller who pointed out that the true joy of life may spring from our hidden and obscure qualities. Tagore was also aware of this and wrote about one's body as a musical instrument – it was the poet's role to play upon its uttermost strings.

Thus the object of the types is not to label and confine people in little boxes; rather it is to let them understand their entire psychological make-up so they can be freed into a much wider heritage.

2. Extraversion and Introversion. Jung devoted much of his book on psychological types to these two attitudes. The Extravert sees objects objectively, that is, it is the object that is most important for them. In contrast the Introvert sees subjectively, so it is their own ideas that are pre-eminent for them. This means that the two see things in an entirely different way. The most obvious result of this can be seen in viewing art. The ordinary verbally dominated Extravert is dismayed and troubled by what they see and do not recognise, and probably never will recognise. Poetry has the same problem: the Extravert writes objectively and the Introvert subjectively, leading to the same incomprehension. The other factors, including two added in the MBTI (judging and perceiving), are subject to the same distortion. All this is a very fruitful area of misunderstanding.

Indeed it was Jung's hope, expressed in the conclusion of his book, that his theory of types might enable people, by understanding the differences, to at least accept, if not fully understand, the thinking of those utterly different from themselves.

He went into historical figures and their lifelong enmities that might have sprung from this source: Tertullian the introverted mystic and Origen the extravert whose thinking is still the basis of some of the Catholic system; the extravert Martin Luther and the introvert Zwingli; Freud extravert and Adler introvert. Others not necessarily enemies were Aristotle and Plato; Goethe the extravert and Schiller introvert; Darwin extravert and Kant introvert.

Jung mentioned some cases to illustrate the problems of understanding between different types. The classic introverted person is the absent-minded professor. Helmholtz the German scientist and genius fitted this description perfectly. He was absolutely useless as a lecturer, having no concept of students' needs and being utterly absorbed in his own theories and ideas. If a student asked a question where only a simple answer was needed to set the student straight, Helmholtz would see all sorts of complications and subtleties, answering the student with subjective and, for the student, incomprehensible jargon.

Jung wrote of another: Gauss, the German scientist called by Laplace the greatest mathematician in Europe, detested giving lectures and would use all sorts of subterfuges to avoid doing it.

Jung singled out the introverted intuitive as being the type most likely to be misunderstood by his fellow beings, especially hard-headed extraverted realists. He wrote that from this type would have come most of the prophets in Scriptures. Nietzsche was one of these whose beautiful ideas were brutally perverted to the Nazi cause.

3. Schiller was concerned with the problem of good and evil in the human mind. His solution was the sense of the beautiful, namely aesthetics. In contrast Jung was of the opinion that what modern man lacked was religion. Religion in the West was mostly delegated to a hierarchy of educated priests who took upon themselves the duty of interceding between the Divine and the congregation, telling the ignorant what they had to do and above all think; such people did not have to think personally about religion.

Later even this tended to break down so that the people were left with practically nothing, not even guidance. Jung thought philosophy too rational and it was not rationality that could cure modern psychological diseases. We had lost the old certainties of religion and its solaces and nothing could replace them – success, progress, increasing material opulence, excitement and entertainment are all as nothing by comparison with this loss of religion.

Jung was taken with Indian thinking and quoted extensively from it. One of the salient characteristics of Eastern religions is that they require personal work; this is seen in the statement of the Buddha: "Work out your own salvation with diligence". In reading Jung, I had to wonder how much of the profound thinking was understood at the time he lived in Europe. Indian thinking is utterly different from Western so that just reading it from a Western point of view is certain to mislead. It is vital that guidance is sought from the great commentaries, especially those written in more recent times, for these are more in tune with Western minds. I mean those written by authorities such as Sri Aurobindo Ghose and Ramana Maharshi, and the most poetic, that of Vinoba Bhave on the *Bhagavadgita*; and that of the European Sri Krishna Prem on the Kathopanishad. Later Shankaracharya and others of the older classic commentators might be read, as well as Aurobindo on the Veda and his tomes on yoga.

I mention this because Jung writes nothing about the two most important ideas; they are Realization, which I have discussed at length, and its derivative Liberation or Freedom (*moksa*, *mukti* and in Zen *satori*). These ideas took the whole of Asia by storm, leading to incomparable joy and the production of great art and immense buildings such as the Stupa at Borobudur in Java of which Tagore wrote a magnificent poem showing how everyone high and low was released by the Great Compassion (*mahakaruna*) and the knowledge that in each one of them was the infinite Being made manifest – all they had to do was remove the dust and grime from their beings. But neither this state of joy nor liberation can be taught, they must be thought out by the individual soul.

This chapter is about the ego. For ordinary practical purposes of life 'Knowing Thyself' is important in the Jungian and Myers-Briggs sense so that people, including oneself, can be understood.

But at the highest level it is more to do with losing or forgetting oneself. But to achieve this is exceedingly difficult; indeed even so great a mystic as Rabindranath Tagore admitted that he never overcame his ego. This battle with the ego has always been recognised in India as being one of the greatest struggles of an aspirant. Mahatma Gandhi referred to the Battle of Kurukshetra in the *Bhagavadgita* as being waged in the mind. It is a personal Armageddon of which most people never become aware; for others the battle consumes a lifetime.

As we saw earlier, all words are illusory in that they never cover the whole subject; this is especially true of the word 'I'. It is the smallest and most harmful word, which we have nurtured throughout our lives. It is a pure self-creation of our ignorance; moreover, it is a trap and acts as a dungeon in which we are chained. Somehow we must transcend it or destroy it.

The real 'I' is something far more profound than this little ego. First we must find out what we really are, that is discover our true bent in life, our essential reason for being and our lifelong purpose. Part of this enquiry entails asking ourselves the old question "What am I?" To search for this logically using words is useless, even harmful, because it will entrench erroneous conceptions of ourselves even deeper. But using Nous, the Higher Intelligence, we can hope for success.

Some people mistakenly think that outside objects of desire can give status, expand their egos and exalt their self-importance. They think further that freedom is being able to do exactly what they like, unrestrained by moral laws. In fact this so-called 'freedom' is enslavement to the desires. Objects of desire can never give freedom, freedom can come only from destroying our desires. Objects of desire are not things in themselves that can be owned – they are a temporary loan, at most a life-rent that sooner or later will be taken from us. To think that true status can be gained by such transitory things is extreme ignorance, and those who judge us by our possessions are as ignorant as we ourselves.

Another harmful effect of the 'I' is to make us suppose that we are separate from all other people and things. This sense of separation and hence isolation is mainly due to verbal thinking, which creates an artificial barrier between ourselves and everything else. The real self is the Universal Light of Consciousness, which is the same in me as in you.

Having absorbed such ideas into the mind, we must go far further. The first ego we develop is small-minded and mean, it is self-serving, boastful, ignorant, in short contemptible. But what it can become is something majestic for the higher ego is linked to the Cosmos. We have to replace the lower ego with a cosmic and creative ego discerned not with ordinary verbal thought but with the cosmic language of intuition.

A Polish friend I met several times in India, Dr. Henryk Skolimowski, lectured about the expansion of the ordinary being until he becomes a Cosmic Being whose mind has broken free from the narrow confines of materialism into the infinite. We must strive to become that Cosmic Being.

Sri Aurobindo, the Seer of Pondicherry in South India, writing about the Supreme Secret of the *Bhagavadgita,* showed that "while there is the truth of the Universalized personality into which we enter by the extinction of ego, without which there is no absolute Liberation or Release, there is another truth of our being as a factor of the highest experience: There is room and infinite room for the heart's love and aspiration illumined and uplifted by knowledge. It is by the perpetual unified closeness of our heart-consciousness, mind-consciousness, that we get the widest, the deepest, the most integral experience of our oneness with the Eternal" (*Essays on the Gita*).

Human intelligence is not simply in the being; much of the mind acts like a receiver in a TV set and is linked to the Cosmic Intelligence, which is tapped into in intuition, meditation and creativity. The ego is like a dead weight that prevents us entering into these wider experiences. It acts as a hobble or anchor that makes us earthbound.

The worlds of creative imagination that we can enter and become part of are among the most beautiful, exalted and joyful experiences a human being can gain. I think of the Gnostics' Orient, the Emerald Cities of Sufism and the strange mathematical world of

Minkowski-Einstein that Korzybski described in *Science and Sanity*. Prophets were said to gain their mystical sayings and visions from meditation in the Ocean of the Transcendent. Visions of midnight hours and reveries come from this "Homeland of the Higher Self" and provide the ravishing joys of mystics. In meditation our minds can enter these regions and leave our small egos far behind with their petty concerns.

An ordinary creative person does not see the endless scope of creativity – they paddle in the shallows at the edge of the ocean, but the person who transcends the ego, the mystic, drowns in that ocean; this is the true Cosmic Being.

Of the two highest aims of Eastern philosophy, I think of Realization as being absolute – you either understand it or you do not. Freedom or Liberation, by contrast, is progressive. It can be at the Stoic level of Epictetus and Diogenes; then the 'Just Being' of Nisargadatta Maharaj, and the losing oneself of Christianity and the 'Letting Go!' of Zen. Next may come the escape from the chains of words, followed by Release (*mukti, moksa*) of India. The final hurdle seems to be the ego, which, it will be recalled, Tagore admitted he never overcame.

If the ego is viewed in the usual verbal way it is almost impossible to transcend, but using Nous it can be done. The Indian word for Nous is *buddhi*, which Sri Krishna Prem wrote was absolutely vital for the spiritual life. All religions have words for it. Sufis speak of *ain* and *ilm ishraq* and *batin*, Christians of *cognito matutina*. All these refer to Higher Intelligence. The ego viewed by Nous is sensed intuitively and becomes a transcendent entity far removed from the petty thing of verbal thought. All that has to be done is to avoid words and in their place use Nous. This is not unlike the avoidance of verbal thought when tackling a problem; words are just as useless for dealing with the ego. Non-Aristotelian Thinking teaches that no words cover the object; the I or ego is always far more than the name we give it.

The Orient and other mystic worlds of the next chapter are only a fraction of this infinite. The real I is not a material thing but a mystic one in which we are joined to all things. We become that infinite ocean of Rumi and we drown in it; rather we ride his 'wooden horse' into that ocean. Here all is visualisation and intu- ition. We are of the creative imagination of Robert Lynd's region beyond the four walls of our material existence. The 'I' of the material world is transcended.

The ego has to be looked at in the same way as we look at all objects; just sensing it and above all 'Letting Go!' and allowing the sub-conscious mind to deal with it. We 'Just Be!'

We do this sensing of the ego by visualising the Universal Light of Consciousness. Reality is structural, hence we can visualise it. We are this Light of Consciousness, which can be likened to a crystal ball of light. More than this, it is a searchlight, which reaches out boundlessly like the light of stars. Consciousness is one of the ulti- mate mysteries that quantum physics tries to understand. It is also the light of vision, evidenced in the visionary recitals of the next chapter, which can be thought of as a vast expansion and devel- opment of the mind. It is about entering these creative regions and becoming a citizen of them.

Mystic religion has always been aware of these worlds – in fact it has all but appropriated them. But though these worlds are not exclusively religious, nonetheless most thought about them has been by mystics, who can be thought of as explorers from whom we can learn much. The Orient and the Sufi Alam al Mithal are mystic examples of these other worlds. To enter them is to leave the mundane world and become a mystic being, an Oriental, whose ego has dispersed in the infinite. The ego is no more, and only when we revert to verbal thought does it and its pettiness manifest again.

Chapter 14
Visionary Recitals, Theophanic Vision and Retirement (Sannyasa)

Before I launch into the subject of this chapter, it has to be emphasised that the Cosmos is a very mysterious place, and it is important that we do not dismiss mystical ideas out of hand. In Sir Roger Penrose's book *Shadows of the Mind*, he goes into the X and Z paradoxes of quantum theory. Here very strange things are to be observed. For instance, Albert Einstein said of one of these paradoxes that it was spooky. He referred to the two atoms of a split particle which despite being far apart, one spinning one way and the other the opposite, when one changes the other responds instantly, defying time and space. Indeed, it is thought possible that these entangled atoms may exist throughout space and be entangled for ever. Our traditional knowledge has little to do with this micro world. We have simply to look and observe as if something before us is utterly new, utterly strange. Similarly, the mystic world is not something that we can apply our experience to; it has to be entered so that it becomes a real experience. Above all the stories of the Visionary Recitals do not come just from imagination, they are real journeys of the soul.

Realization as taught by Krishnamurti is either understood or it is not; there is no half-way house. Usually it comes suddenly as a revelation reminiscent of the way a creative breakthrough occurs in science after a period of incubation; or indeed how Korzybski's Non-Aristotelian Thinking is mastered. The verbal illusion in which most of the world is held captive dissolves and that person will never see things as they had learned to see them. This creates an absolute division of mankind. The Realized person looks at fellow beings and cannot understand why they do not see what, to them, is clear. Nor can their fellow beings ever be aware of the beauty and delight the Realized person possesses. Tagore felt wonder that no one could see the joy that was almost bursting forth from within him. I think a Sufi had a similar experience when he said that God had placed a moon in his soul that would never set.

111

Of this blindness of mankind Rumi wrote: "Do Thou O God show unto us everything as it really is in this house of illusion." In the same way aspirants seeking Realization should pray like this: "May we regain the vision we had of the world as it was when we were children: everything as wordless pictures of light."

Non-Aristotelian Thinking is about using another dimension of the mind, not the verbal, rational thought of every day. Using it the mystic can go on to the worlds of vision, which are some of the most beautiful ideas ever conceived by the human mind. This is so because they come from the conjunction of creativity and divine beauty. This supreme beauty was part of the teaching of Ibnal-Arabi. For him the sensing of divine beauty in an object was to see with theophanic vision, that is to see the divine in the object, which is always accompanied by rapture. He used the analogy of the collar or ring of the ringdove which represents the covenant that exists between the Creator and the creature. The plaintive call "coo, coo", "Where? Where?" symbolises the spiritual seeker's quest for the divine. This beauty comes from the Collective Unconscious, the morphogenetic field and the Sufi Alam al Mithal, etc. Here are to be found the courts of Gandharva kings and the Emerald Cities.

Poets have conceived of supremely beautiful regions such as Peach Blossom Spring in China, Land of the Ever Young of the Celts, Shangri La, Eldorado, and so on. But compared to them mystic poetry and the Visionary Recitals are of a higher order. Much of this mystic poetry was composed in trances, such as Rumi's poems of the *Divan of Shams Y Tabriz*. These were written down by his disciples while Rumi was reciting and turning round a pillar of his house, lost to the world. These were divinely inspired poems, which may be called theophanies; no other poetry can compare with them.

Like the twelve Just Men of Jewish tradition that are said to exist in every generation, there seems to be a certain number of every generation that see the illusion of life described in the image of Plato's Cave, where the shadows are seen as reality. It is an amazing mystery why the human race has been unable to see the verbal illusion despite this being pointed out for the last 2,000 to 3,000 years. Seers have sought to pass on this message to their fellow beings. Sometimes, it is passed on openly as in Hinduism and Buddhism. Sometimes because of persecution, it is disguised. But either way it has not been very clear. Only Korzybski it seems, who knew little about Eastern thought, has formulated a truly rational exposition of it.

In Europe and the Middle East it can be seen in the Visionary Recitals. Of these the example that puts its message very clearly and explains the terms Orient (spiritual) and Occident (material) is the *Song of the Pearl* discussed earlier in this book. It will be recalled that a young prince is sent from the Orient to the Occident to bring back the Pearl without price. He arrives in Egypt, the material world, and is fed the food of forgetfulness. This is the state of human beings who do not see reality or the spiritual world; it is also the meaning of *gnosis* – the knowledge of this state, and it is the theme of most Visionary Recitals. The prince then receives a letter brought by an eagle signed by his father and by his mother, the Queen of the Orient. He now understands his state and sets out to return to the Orient.

Religions have many stories on this same theme of our origin in the Orient and the leaving from the Occident. In Europe and the Middle East they were called Visionary Recitals; this term was used because each is a spiritual journey described by the mystic, hence it is a personal recital. Most of these entail a pilgrim entering a reverie at which time he is confronted by a guide, an angel or Nous, who is the initiator for the visionary journey.

Persians believed that human beings came from the light; they were creatures of the light who were obscured by the darkness of matter. More than this, they were creatures of the beyond and not of the material world at all. The word 'orientation' is used to denote this state in which people recognise that they do not belong to the terrestrial world but are orientated to another. Furthermore, this word Orient is interchangeable in meaning with North, which is not of a horizontal but a vertical pole. These words have nothing to do with our geography books – rather they refer to maps of a mental and spiritual Orient. Orientation is fundamental to all life in that people are aware of their position in the world and where the physical North and other compass points are. But they are lost when it comes to spiritual orientation, leading to a division of mankind into materiaiststs – Occidentals and mystics – Orientals.

The history of an invisible spiritual mankind whose cycles of earthly pilgrimage refer to events in heaven is part of all mystic thinking, for it is to be found in the Zoroastrians, Manicheans, Hermatists, Sufis, Sabeans of Harran and in Christian Gnosis as well as in Tao and among Buddhists of Central Asia; moreover it appears in poetry, philosophy and ancient legends. In the book of Hermes Trismegistus, Phos is the Being of Light and Adam, his double, is the creature of the Earth. Phos was innocent and peaceful, and pre-existed in Paradise, but he was tricked into clothing himself in the body of corporeal Adam. In the Christian Gnostics' version of Christ's ascension and resurrection, Christ was the Man of Light who spoke to Mary Magdalene when she acted as an intermediary between the disciples and Christ's resurrected Being. These ideas are so fundamental a part of human thought that innumerable stories have been passed down from antiquity about them. One of the earliest was Mazdean (Zoroastrian):

> Zarathustra yearned for his spiritual home and set out with some companions of both sexes; he reached the Cosmic Mountain called the Mountain of the Dawns, from whose summit the Bridge Chinvat springs forth to span the passage to the Beyond. To yearn for Eran Vej, the Mazdean Paradise, is to long for the Earth of Vision, it is to reach the Heavenly Earth where the meeting takes place with the Holy Immortals. The Mountain of Vision is the psychocosmic Mountain seen as homologous with the human microcosm. This is the same Mountain of the Dawns, where the being meets his higher self, his Angel. Zarathustra is enjoined to cast off his robe, which is his material body and organs of sensory perception, because in Eran Vej it is the subtle body of light that is the seat and organs of events.
>
> (from Henry Corbin, *The Man of Light in Iranian Sufism*)

Avicenna (Ibn Sina) wrote three Visionary Recitals. The first, *Hayy Ibn Yaqzan*, was the introduction to his second, *The Story of the Bird*, which is similar to the better known *Parliament of the Birds of Attar*. The third of Avicenna's trilogy was *Salaman and Absal*, which was about the two parts of the soul represented by Salaman and Absal as lovers. Absal has to die in order for the soul to be integrated. All these stories give insights into the working of the mind so they are 'real' stories, that is experiences of the mind.

Hayy Ibn Yaqzan was used by Yahya Suhrawardi as the initiation for his *A Tale of Occidental Exile*. In this Recital Suhrawardi and his companions descend into the Occident from the Orient. They are surrounded and taken bound in shackles and fetters of iron (the body) and imprisoned at the bottom of the deepest well (the dark world). Here is the same ignorance and slavery of human beings.

In another version, the pilgrim escapes from the pit or well (the world) and climbs the Sacred Mountain Qaf where he finds the Emerald Cities of Jabalqa and Jabarsa.

One of the Mazdean stories concerned Yima the Beautiful who was told to build a Var or enclosure where the best of mortals would live secure from the demonic powers unleashed on the world. It had a gate and luminous windows, which themselves secreted an inner light. Light was associated with the divine and matter with the demonic powers. Persian miniature paintings demonstrated this, for they had no shadows so that they would depict the wonder of light in a shadowless land. In the same way in Turkey Byzantine mosaic cubes were reinforced with gold and precious metals for the purpose of depicting pure light.

Inhabitants of these shadowless lands were Beings of Light; examples are Hyperboreans, people of the Northern Lights. Another group, the Mandeans, believed in an intermediate world separated from the rest of mankind by an immense mountain of ice.

Rumi wrote two stories that are similar to Visionary Recitals. To him the sea or ocean denoted the spiritual world. He used the analogy of a hen fostering a brood of ducklings. To her amazement the ducklings took to water, for they were mystics. He described the mystic life as a journey on horseback as far as the ocean but after that a wooden horse was needed. He wrote: "The footprints are as on the shore of the Ocean and they become naught. The resting places for the travellers on dry land are houses and villages and caravanserais, but on the Ocean there is no floor or roof. The Oceanic stages have no visible beacon, they have no sign or name" (*Mathnawi*).

Rumi wrote the story of the Three Princes, which is one of the most profound in the *Mathnawi*. Some of his Western translators seemed to think he had lost some of his powers when he wrote these two stories near the end of his life at 68 years of age. I cannot agree with them. The last two books of the *Mathnawi* dealt with the final aims of the mystic and had in them more profound thinking; indeed their beautiful ideas were even more numerous than in the four earlier books. I have always regarded this fact as an indication that for the mystic there is no end to the creative life.

The King (God) ordered his three sons to go out and inspect the kingdom, but on no account were they to enter a certain fortress. The Princes ignored the order and entered the fortress, which was a hall of pictures. They fell in love with the portrait of the Emperor of China's daughter. The hall of pictures is the phenomenal world, which is seen in ecstasy by mystics; the Emperor of China's daughter is divine beauty seen only by those who have died to self.

In India also are stories of these visionary worlds. For instance, the Gandharvas live in a solar world where the same green of the Emerald Cities suffuses the landscape. Sri Krishna Prem (Ronald Nixon) wrote of the Gandharvas:

> The Gandharva is the Higher Self and the land of the Gandharvas is on the plane of Higher Mind. The Gandharva can be perceived as having the same quality as the body of a man seen within the clear green waters of a mountain lake. The outline may wave and flicker with the movement of unseen currents but there can be no doubt as to the identity of the form, to which indeed the transparent waters impart a certain crystalline glamour making the man a dweller of another world. In this higher world all is bathed in an emerald radiance, an impersonal crystalline brightness, a thrice distilled clarity of cool and magic light, which will be recognised as similar in character to the magical beauty of objects seen in the water of a rocky pool.

The Buddha himself spoke of such a scene: "Just, O King, as if in a mountain fastness there were a pool of water, clear, translucent and serene; and a man, standing on the bank and with eyes to see should perceive the oysters and the shells, the gravel and the pebbles and the shoals of fish as they move about or lie within it" (*Dialogues on the Fruits of the Life of a Recluse*).

Another Far Eastern example of a visionary world is that described by D. T. Suzuki, a famous Zen scholar, writing about the Gandavyuha of the Avatamsaka Sutra on the entry into the Dharmadhatu: "When we come to the Gandavyuha we find nothing cold, nothing grey or earth-coloured and nothing humanly mean; for everything one touches in the Gandavyuha shines out in an unsurpassable manner; we are miraculously lifted among the heavenly galaxies ..." "In the Gandavyuha there is no shadowiness ..." (*Essays in Zen Buddhism*).

In India life is divided into four parts – the child, the student, the householder and finally *Sannyasa*, or retirement. Contrary to Western ideas, the first three are preliminaries to the last, which is the crown and culmination of life. Many people in the West think that retirement is to stop work and play for the rest of life, turning it into an adult childhood. *Sannyasa* is not like that at all. The *Sannyasi*, the practiser of *Sannyasa*, enters the real world and for them it is a rebirth of the soul. This is a kind of miracle of the spiritual so that what went before is erased; indeed many people who were the least in the material world become the most exalted in the spiritual world – one only has to think of Raidas the Sweeper and Kabir the Weaver.

We should believe in the limitless potential of retirement. It is at the least an opportunity for physical freedom from the economic, intellectual and social chains and for the entry into a cosmic existence.

Tagore wrote how the aspirant can always go further, whether this is during *Sannyasa* or earlier:

> I thought that my voyage had come to its end at the last limits of my power, that the path before me was closed, that provisions were exhausted and the time come to take shelter in a silent obscurity.

> But I find that thy will knows no end in me. And when old words die out on the tongue, new melodies break forth from the heart; and where the old tracks are lost, new country is revealed with its wonders.
>
> (*Collected Poems and Plays*)

For an ordinary Aristotelian thinker what I have written in this chapter may seem like illusory escape mechanisms. But the Cave of Plato* with its prisoners is much more than a depiction of the illusion of life. The prisoners are trapped in the lower part of the Structural Differential, that is, they are restricted to what is in their memories and what their minds can grasp within the boundaries of their filter mechanisms. Their thinking is a dreary rummaging among old ideas, or if they do come upon a new idea it has to be within their limits of acceptable ideas. Hence most of the universe with its mystery is beyond bounds. In contrast Realized beings throw off their chains of words and memory and are freed into the infinite Cosmos with its wonder and beauty.

The cave of Plato is not just about Release; the climb by the prisoners to the light and sun is a kind of visionary journey. More than that, it is a vast expansion of the mind into new dimensions.

A woman, a spiritual friend of mine, a teacher at Delhi University, whom I have never met face to face, wrote to me that this kind of writing is a *Satsang*. A *Satsang* is a sort of spiritual concert or, for me, a *Sadhana* or spiritual worship. I was reminded that of the many paths of religion this one is called the Sunlit Path of joy and delight. In fact with creativity it is the Elixir of Life.

When I think of mysticism, I am carried away from the ignorance and greed of materialism and I go with Raidas the Sweeper and Kabir the Weaver into the enchanted gardens where Rumi and Li Po and Kalidas sing for ever.

It was said of Ramakrishna of Calcutta that no one who went to him ever returned to the world. This can be said with even more truth of those who enter the mystic world, for they become Orientals who have gone to their original home. They also never come back to the world.

Sannyasa should also be about never coming back to the world. It must be the time when all demands and obligations cease, so it

---

* In a note, I wrote how Plato is regarded in the East as a mystic and Realized being. In fact the greatest philosopher of Islam, Ibnal-Arabi, was given the name Son of Plato. Ibnal-Arabi wrote of how in his youth he was 'veiled' and the way in which he became 'unveiled'. The image of the Cave indicates that Plato was also 'unveiled'.

should be a final liberation. It is surely another of the great spiritual ideas of India, ranking only a little below Realization and Liberation. It is a renewal of life, a revolution in the whole way of living, indeed a rebirth of the soul; moreover it is an emancipation from the tyranny of ignorant opinion that is often of the abjectness of old age.

This book can be used as a preparation for *Sannyasa*. Externally our existence should be like Thoreau's life of rapture, which epitomises *Sannyasa*; he described it as a prolonged youth.* Looked at in another way it is like the climb of the prisoners of Plato's Cave into the sunlight of reality, which can give a vision of sublime wonder and exaltation. Internally there is an even more wonderful vision, a world of pictures made of light in which mankind can be journeyers on visionary voyages.

And this is not all there is. Mystic philosophy can solve all problems of human happiness. The escape I write about is noted in Ancient Wisdom and the Mystery Ceremonies, where the body is described as a tomb or sepulchre. This is the real death, the living death of a human being bound in ignorance. Only after transformation or Realization is there escape into the infinite.

David Bohm complained that most scientists in the period of learning up to their graduation laid down a paradigm, a system and method of scientific thought that acted as a straitjacket preventing their seeing beyond their paradigm. Similarly, most people of the world have a paradigm, like a parapet, that prevents their seeing. The view beyond the parapet is incomparably more magnificent than any physical view. But these people are stuck between the parameters of their minds. Their thought is petrified or fossilised in their memories, so they live on old ideas: in other words they live in the past. By contrast, for perception-dominated thinkers life is an endless search or exploration of new things and new ideas.

Meditation is thought beyond the paradigm or parapet. It is the breaking out from the four walls of Robert Lynd into the worlds of

Thoreau described his life as a prolonged youth. His Journal records this delight and rapture of creativity on almost every page. In contrast, most people's lives are a prolonged old age starting in youth.

poetry and creativity. In meditation *Sannyasis* can become perpetual explorers of the Cosmos, their bodies being no more than launch pads for the journey. They leave the ordinary mundane world far behind them. All verbal concepts, even the fear of death, cannot survive in the rarefied air of those distant and beautiful regions of the Visionary Recitals.

Indians speak of Para Nirvana, the Far Nirvana, meaning death. *Sannyasis* can go on to *Para Sannyasa*, an ultimate liberation, though it must be added that in mysticism there is no ultimate end; rather it is an endless unfolding of more and more wonderful experiences.

Para Sannyasa entails for me becoming a Cosmic Being, a spiritual explorer beyond the horizons of memory; a creative adventurer and mystic.

Mysticism is the religion of poets, ecstatic lovers, artists and musicians. As Plotinus wished, let the last word here belong to whoever possesses the soul of a lover, of a philosopher and of a musician.

As one who desires and hopes for those wondrous experiences and joys of mystics, I wish to end with a few lines I wrote on the harvests of *Sannyasa*:

> I saw the golden rivers of the wheat,
> The horses and the harvesters toiling
> On the great canvases of the fields,
> The people banding and sheaving the harvest.
>
> But the horses were spectral,
> The men and fields were illusions,
> Only the harvest was real,
> A brilliant unearthly harvest.
>
> And there at the end of my days,
> I near the fields of the mystics.
> I see dreams of millennial seers
> Fast ripening into shining harvests.

Bibliography

Ansoff, H. Igor. *Corporate Strategy.* Penguin, 1965.

Arberry, A. J. *Discourses of Rumi.* John Murray, 1961.

Arberry, A. J. *Mystical Poems of Rumi.* University of Chicago Press, 1968.

Bayne, Rowan. *Myers-Briggs Type Indicator.* Stanley Thorne, 1995.

Bohm, David and Peat, F. D. *Science Order and Creativity.* Routledge, 1987.

Corbin, Henry. *The Man of Light in Iranian Sufism.* Trans. Nancy Pearson. Shambala, 1978.

Corbin, Henry. *Avicenna and the Visionary Recital.* Trans. Willard Trask. Spring Publications, Inc., 1986.

Corbin, Henry. *Creative Imagination in the Sufism of Ibnal-Arabi.* Trans. Ralph Manheim. Princeton, 1969.

Crowther, J. A. *Michael Faraday.* Macmillan, 1920.

De Bono, Edward. *The Five Day Course in Thinking.* Pelican, 1967.

Epictetus. *Epictetus.* Trans. W. A. Oldfather. Heinemann Loeb, 1925.

Epictetus. *Moral Discourses and Enchiridion.* Trans. Elizabeth Carter. J. M. Dent and E. P. Dutton, 1910.

Eysenck, Hans. *Genius.* Cambridge, 1995.

Falconar, A. E. I. *Gardens of Meditation.* Colin Smythe, 1980.

Falconar, A. E. I. *How to Use Your Nous.* Non-Aristotelian Publishing, 1986.

Falconar, A. E. I. *Sufi Literature and the Journey to Immortality.* Non-Aristotelian Publishing, 1991.

Falconar, A. E. I. *Realization, Enlightenment and the Life of Rapture.* Non-Aristotelian Publishing, 1994.

Gide, André. *Fruits of the Earth (Les Nourritures Terrestres).* Penguin, 1949 (originally published 1897).

Gordon, W. J. J. *Synectics.* Harper & Row, 1961.

Herrigel, Eugen. *Zen in the Art of Archery.* Routledge, 1953.

Hoffmann, Yoel. *The Sound of the One Hand.* Paladin, 1977.

Jung, Carl Gustav. *Psychological Types.* Trans. H. G. Baynes. Kegan Paul, 1926.

Kingsley, P. *In the Dark Places of Wisdom.* Element, 1999.

Krishna Khosla. *The Sufism of Rumi.* Element, 1987.

Koestler, Arthur. *Act of Creation.* Picador, 1964.

Korzybski, Alfred. *Science and Sanity.* Institute of General Semantics, 1974.

Krishnamurti, J. *Commentaries on Living.* Gollancz, 1960.

Lincoln, James. *Incentive Management.* Lincoln. Co. Publication, 1951.

Lowes, J. L. *The Road to Xanadu.* Houghton Mifflin, 1927.

Lynd, Robert. *Introduction to An Anthology of Modern Verse.* Methuen, 1921.

Maslow, Abraham H. *Motivation and Personality.* Harper & Row, 1970.

Penrose, Sir Roger. *Shadows of the Mind.* Oxford, 1994.

Plato. *Dialogues.* Trans. B. Jowett. Oxford, 1971.

Popper, Sir Karl. *The Logic of Scientific Discovery.* Routledge, 1959.

Popper, Sir Karl. *All Life is Problem Solving: The Unended Quest.* Routledge, 1974.

Popper, Sir Karl. *The World of Parmenides.* Routledge, 1998.

Rosenau, Helen. *E. L. Boullée and Visionary Architecture.* Academy/Harmony, 1976.

Rumi, Jalaluddin. *Mathnawi.* Trans. R. A. Nicholson. Luzac, E. W. Gibb Memorial, 1960.

Seneca. *Moral Essays.* Trans. J. W. Basore. Heinemann Loeb, 1935.

Sheldrake, Rupert. *A New Science of Life* (new edition). Parkstreet, USA, 1999.

Sri Aurobindo. *On the Veda.* Aurobindo Ashram, 1956.

Sri Aurobindo. *Essays on the Gita.* Aurobindo Ashram, 1959.

Sri Krishna Prem. *The Yoga of the Kathopanishad.* New Order Books, India, 1982.

Sri Nisargadatta Maharaj. *I Am That.* Trans. Maurice Frydman. Chetana, 1973.

Sri Ramakrishna. *The Great Master, The Gospel of Ramakrishna.* Ramakrishna, Madras, 1944.

Suzuki, D. T. *Essays in Zen Buddhism.* Rider, 1958.

Tagore, Rabindranath. *Creative Unity.* Macmillan, 1922.

Tagore, Rabindranath. *The Religion of Man.* The Hibbert Lectures for 1930. Allen & Unwin, 1931.

Tagore, Rabindranath. *Collected Poems and Plays.* Macmillan, 1958.

Tagore, Rabindranath (trans.). *100 Poems of Kabir.* Macmillan, 1962.

Thoreau, Henry David. *Journal.* Dover, 1962.

Vinoba Bhave. *Talks on the Gita.* George Allen & Unwin, 1956.

Watson, James D. *The Double Helix.* Penguin, 1970.

Weber, Renee. *Dialogues with Scientists and Sages.* Routledge, 1986.

Young, J. Z. *Programs of the Brain.* Oxford, 1978.

Index

Crown House Publishing
www.crownhouse.co.uk

Me, Myself, My Team
How To Become An Effective Team Player Using NLP

Angus McLeod, PhD

In *Me, Myself, My Team*, Angus McLeod looks at the team within each of us, and at each of us as part of a team. Providing a wealth of ideas to help the reader find new perceptions and new courses of action, *Me, Myself, My Team* asks the questions:

- ◆ WHO is leading?
- ◆ WHO is following?

- ◆ WHERE are we pro-active?
- ◆ WHERE are we reluctant?

- ◆ HOW does the commentary inside our head get in the way of effective communication with others?

By answering these questions with acute observations, *Me, Myself, My Team* sets the success criteria for high performing teams, and calculates effective solutions that will make a difference in both communication and motivation. Having its foundation in the belief that *openness and flexibility are the primary keys to personal effectiveness*, it promotes the need for *real* empowerment of the self – and not the so-called 'empowerment' bestowed by senior managers. Upbeat, friendly and full of practical ideas, this is an exceptional management book that demonstrates how we really can achieve the greatest success by being a team player.

PAPERBACK   132 PAGES   ISBN:1899836381

USA & Canada *orders to:*
Crown House Publishing
P.O. Box 2223, Williston, VT 05495-2223, USA
Tel: 877-925-1213, Fax: 802-864-7626
E-mail: info@CHPUS.com
www.CHPUS.com

UK & Rest of World *orders to:*
The Anglo American Book Company Ltd.
Crown Buildings, Bancyfelin, Carmarthen, Wales SA33 5ND
Tel: +44 (0)1267 211880/211886, Fax: +44 (0)1267 211882
E-mail: books@anglo-american.co.uk
www.anglo-american.co.uk

Australasia *orders to:*
Footprint Books Pty Ltd.
Unit 4/92A Mona Vale Road, Mona Vale NSW 2103, Australia
Tel: +61 (0) 2 9997 3973, Fax: +61 (0) 2 9997 3185
E-mail: info@footprint.com.au
www.footprint.com.au

Singapore *orders to:*
Publishers Marketing Services Pte Ltd.
10-C Jalan Ampas #07-01
Ho Seng Lee Flatted Warehouse, Singapore 329513
Tel: +65 6256 5166, Fax: +65 6253 0008
E-mail: info@pms.com.sg
www.pms.com.sg

Malaysia *orders to:*
Publishers Marketing Services Pte Ltd
Unit 509, Block E, Phileo Damansara 1, Jalan 16/11
46350 Petaling Jaya, Selangor, Malaysia
Tel : 03 7955 3588, Fax : 03 7955 3017
E-mail: pmsmal@po.jaring.my
www.pms.com.sg

South Africa *orders to:*
Everybody's Books
Box 201321 Durban North 401, 1 Highdale Road,
25 Glen Park, Glen Anil 4051, KwaZulu NATAL, South Africa
Tel: +27 (0) 31 569 2229, Fax: +27 (0) 31 569 2234
E-mail: ebbooks@iafrica.com